LEADERSHIP
SUCCESS
in 10 MINUTES
a DAY

BOB PHILLIPS

HARVEST HOUSE PUBLIS
EUGENE, OREGON

D1118508

Cover by Bryce Williamson

Cover photo © Plisman / Gettyimages

For bulk, special sales, or ministry purchases, please call 1-800-547-8979. Email: Customerservice@hhpbooks.com

Leadership Success in 10 Minutes a Day
Copyright © 2020 by Bob Phillips
Published by Harvest House Publishers
Eugene, Oregon 97408
www.harvesthousepublishers.com

ISBN 978-0-7369-8143-9 (pbk)
ISBN 978-0-7369-8144-6 (eBook)

Library of Congress Cataloging-in-Publication Data

Names: Phillips, Bob, author.
Title: Leadership success in 10 minutes a day / Bob Phillips.
Other titles: Leadership success in ten minutes a day
Description: Eugene, Oregon : Harvest House Publishers, 2020. | Summary:
   "Whether you are a first-time leader or have been in a position of
   authority for many years, Bob Phillips will help you gain a vision for
   the kind of leader you want to be and learn to leverage your authority
   when you lead by example"—Provided by publisher.
Identifiers: LCCN 2020012304 (print) | LCCN 2020012305 (ebook) | ISBN
   9780736981439 (trade paperback) | ISBN 9780736981446 (ebook)
Subjects: LCSH: Leadership—Religious aspects—Christianity.
Classification: LCC BV4597.53.L43 P49 2020 (print) | LCC BV4597.53.L43
   (ebook) | DDC 253--dc23
LC record available at https://lccn.loc.gov/2020012304
LC ebook record available at https://lccn.loc.gov/2020012305

Printed in the United States of America

21 22 23 24 25 26 27 28 / BP-RD / 10 9 8 7 6 5 4 3 2

Contents

The Life Cycle of Every Organization

Tools for Every Leader

Finding Success as a Leader

What is leadership all about? The term *lead* implies a number of concepts. It can mean to guide by holding the hand or to direct and show the way as a guide. To some it means to proceed or to introduce by going first. By leading one may induce, cause, or influence actions by other people. Leading often refers to conduct as a chief commander or to hold first place in a rank. A leader is a person who directs or commands by words or leads personally by their actions.

In *boxing*, the lead is to strike the first blow. In *theater*, the lead is the principle or person in the main role. In *journalism*, a lead is the opening line. In *music*, the lead is the conductor or the lead tone. In *law*, a lead refers to the case that determines the law. In *cards*, to lead is to have the right to play first. In *aeronautics*, the leading edge is the foremost part of the wing or propeller blade. A *leading question* is worded specifically to suggest the desired answer, which opens the way for further questions. Basically, the concept of *lead* is to be first or to be in front.

The Pointman Leadership Institute gives five definitions of leadership.

1. The ability to clearly understand and articulate the goal.

2. The confidence to be out in front and show the way to the goal.

3. The ability to convince people to follow as an act of their free choice.

4. The desire to help people develop and pursue excellence.

5. The ability to inspire people to achieve their full potential.

The goal is number three: the ability to convince people to follow as an act of their own free choice. How is that to be accomplished? The answer is simple. If you do numbers one, two, four, and five, people will follow you as an act of their own free will.

When it comes to leadership success, various authors offer suggestions. Jack Welch says, "Before you are a leader, success is all about growing yourself. When you become a leader, success is all about growing others." Booker T. Washington commented, "I have learned that success is to be measured not so much by the position that one has reached in life as by the obstacles which he has had to overcome while trying to succeed." A.W. Tozer conveyed a little different thought when he said, "God may allow His servant to succeed when He has disciplined him to a point where he does not need to succeed to be happy. The man who is elated by success and cast down by failure is still a carnal man. At best his fruit will have a worm in it."

Napoleon Hill talks about both success and defeat. "Before success comes in any man's life, he is sure to meet with much temporary defeat, and, perhaps some failure. When defeat overtakes a man, the easiest and most logical thing to do is to quit. That is exactly what the majority of men do."

Leadership Success in 10 Minutes a Day is a collection of thoughts about leadership written for both first-time and seasoned leaders. These thoughts can be read in ten minutes or less and then put into practice. The concepts are designed to alert you, encourage you, and challenge you not to quit as a leader. They are to help you be certain that your leadership ladder is leaning against the right wall.

> *Better to love God and die unknown*
> *than to love the world and be a hero;*
> *Better to be content with poverty*
> *than to die a slave to wealth;*
> *Better to have taken some risks and lost*
> *than to have done nothing and succeeded at it;*
> *Better to have lost some battles*
> *than to have retreated from the war;*

Better to have failed when serving God
than to have succeeded when serving the devil.
What a tragedy to climb the ladder of success only to discover
that the ladder was leaning against the wrong wall.

Erwin W. Lutzer

QUALITIES EVERY LEADER NEEDS

1

Essential Traits of a Great Leader

*Leadership is not about a title or a designation.
It's about impact, influence and inspiration.
Impact involves getting results, influence
is about spreading the passion you have
for your work, and you have to inspire
teammates and customers.*

Robin S. Sharma

The Board of Directors for the Carmello Corporation was facing a very strategic decision. The CEO and founder George Carmello had a heart attack while on the golf course. He was immediately sent to the hospital but passed away after three days. Everyone was in shock. George was only 56 years old, and no one had thought about any succession plan to replace him in case of an accident or death.

The Board of Directors now faced the issue of choosing a new CEO. They considered the pros and cons of selecting someone from within the corporation or seeking an outsider to lead the company. They leaned toward someone within who was familiar with the operation, feeling that it would take too much time to get a new leader from the outside up to speed.

The chairman of the Board asked the other members what they thought they should look for in choosing a new leader. They began to brainstorm some qualities they considered necessary.

One of the members said, "I think the most important quality would be that of *character*. We need someone who is a person of integrity. He or she needs to be honest and straightforward. The Board, the staff, and our customers need to have someone they can trust. This is an absolutely necessary foundation."

> Character isn't something you were born with and
> can't change like your fingerprints. It's something
> you weren't born with and must take
> responsibility for forming.
>
> ~ JIM ROHN

A second board member added, "I think the next quality we should look for is that of *competence*. There's no question that they should be a person of character. But you know it's possible to be a person of character and a nice guy, but not competent in the area of leadership that's needed. Our new leader needs to have the skills necessary to lead our company into the future. You wouldn't take someone who's only experience was in washing windows and put them in charge of hundreds of employees and a budget in the millions of dollars. We need to have someone who has a track record for leading people and understanding our market. They need to be capable and have a capacity to handle important decision-making. And they need to be creative."

> Competence goes beyond words.
> It's the leader's ability to say it,
> plan it, and do it in such a way that you know how—
> and know that they want to follow you.
>
> ~ JOHN MAXWELL

If you think you can do it, that's confidence.
If you do it, that's competence.

"I agree with what has been suggested so far," said another board member. "I would like to add that I think our next leader needs to have a *calling* to the position as CEO for the Carmello Corporation. Character is foundational, competence is essential, but a calling seems to add a caring for what we do...a concern for leading our people...and a commitment to the job and tasks that are needed. We want someone who is interested in what we do and where we are going. We need a leader who desires to make an impact."

God's calling requires action.
When God calls you, he calls collect...
you better be willing to accept the charges of your calling.

~ STEVE MARABOLI

A fourth board member chimed in, "The mention of leadership *character, competence*, and *calling* is right on. We need them in our next leader. I think I would like to add the word *chemistry*. Our new leader needs to have a psychological and relational personality that communicates compassion, caring, and a charisma with our staff, our customers, and our suppliers. People need to be able to like and relate to our new leader."

Sometimes you meet a person and just click—
you're comfortable with them,
like you've known them your whole life,
and you don't have to pretend to be anyone or anything.

~ALEXANDRA ANDRONETTO

Like great teams in sports and business endeavors,
if there's a chemistry among the participants, and they
truly enjoy fellowship together, everybody wants to be there,
stay involved, and just have fun together.

~ ED GREENWOOD

"I couldn't agree with you all any more about the four qualities needed in our next leader. I would only suggest one more. That's the trait of *conviction*. People want to follow someone who has done their homework with critical thinking and has confidence in the direction they're going. Our employees and our customers need someone who is courageous and willing to make tough decisions. *Conviction* gives the leader an aura or distinctive quality that is picked up by others. It's seen in the way they carry themselves. The way they talk. It's a

type of command presence that creates trust and confidence in them as a leader."

> Strong convictions precede
> great actions.
>
> ~JAMES FREEMAN CLARKE

> One man with conviction will
> overwhelm a hundred who only have opinions.
>
> ~ WINSTON CHURCHILL

> Hold strong to your convictions.
> Remain humble in your speech.
> Let your actions tell your story.
>
> ~POPE FRANCIS

> Be attractive and winsome, but do not
> compromise your convictions for the sake of popularity.
>
> ~BILLY GRAHAM

> Belief is something you will argue about.
> A conviction is something you will die for.
>
> ~ HOWARD HENDRICKS

All Scripture is God-breathed [given by divine inspiration] and is profitable for instruction, for conviction [of sin], for correction [of error and restoration to obedience], for training in righteousness [learning to live in conformity to God's will, both publicly and privately—behaving honorably with personal integrity and moral courage]; so that the man of God may be complete *and* proficient, outfitted *and* thoroughly equipped for every good work (2 Timothy 3:16-17).

Dear Lord, ⎯⎯⎯⎯⎯⎯⎯⎯⎯⎯⎯⎯⎯⎯⎯⎯⎯⎯

Help me to become a person with integrity and strong character. I want You and others to be able to trust me. Help me to develop competence in the areas for which I have been entrusted. Give me the assurance that I'm in the calling You have designed me for. Help me to be concerned and compassionate and develop a chemistry with the people under my leadership. Give me the conviction, confidence, and courage to become an effective leader that brings You glory and honor.

Amen

LEADERSHIP SUCCESS

The two most important days in your life are the day you were born and the day you find out why.

MARK TWAIN

2

Staying on Track

*Who decides what is right and wrong in the world? Who has the
authority to define morality for all creation? It is not the courts,
congress, the media, public opinion, the "politically correct"
police, the "tolerance" brigade or even the church. The
only answer has been, is and always will be Jesus Christ.
You can find His opinion on a great variety of
subjects in His bestseller...the Bible.*

JEFFREY E. RAMSEY

In Greek mythology, Atalanta was a beautiful woman with many skills
and abilities. She was an avid hunter and she loved to run swiftly. She
would often run races against men and would always come out the vic-
tor—which damaged the ego and pride of many men.

However, she began to be bored with the running ability of men.
There was little challenge in running against them. She thought to herself, *"Maybe they would run faster and give me more of a challenge if there
was some type of reward for winning the race."* She then put out a challenge to all men that if they could beat her in a race, then she would
marry the one who won. But, if they lost the race, they would have
their heads cut off.

Because of Atalanta's great beauty, many men attempted to win her
hand in marriage. And many men lost the race and their heads. This
still happens today. Many men lose their heads over the attraction to
a beautiful girl.

One day a friend of Hippomenes said, "Hippomenes, you are the
fastest runner I have ever seen. You should try to win the race against
Atalanta."

"No," Hippomenes responded. "Who would want to risk his neck for some girl!"

The friend replied, "Have you seen her?"

A little time passed until one day Hippomenes caught his first glimpse of Atalanta. He couldn't believe his eyes. She was stunning. He was immediately drawn to the possibility of winning her hand in marriage. He signed up for the challenge.

Hippomenes knew that he would have to run his hardest to win. He was also smart enough to know he would need a little help besides just his running ability. With this in mind, he went to a friend who was a goldsmith and commissioned three beautiful golden apples.

On the day of the race, Hippomenes hid the three golden apples in his tunic. The officials started the race and both he and Atalanta took off running at great speed. For a while Hippomenes kept up with Atalanta, but because he was carrying three heavy golden apples, he began to drop behind her. She glanced back and smiled, thinking, *"This will be easy."*

Then Hippomenes reached into his tunic and took out one of the golden apples. He tossed it alongside the path where Atalanta was running. Out of the corner of her eye, she noticed a shiny object roll by her. She stopped to see what it was, reached down and picked it up, and began to admire it.

Who do you think ran by while she was looking at the apple?

It took a moment for her to realize that Hippomenes had gained some distance. A little more time still and she caught him, retaking the lead.

Soon after they had passed the halfway mark of the race, Hippomenes reached into his tunic and withdrew the second golden apple. This time he tossed the apple a little further off the race path. Again Atalanta saw a shiny object roll by. She thought, *If one golden apple was good, then two of them would be twice as good.* She began thinking about where she would place them in her home.

Who do you think ran by while she was looking at the apples?

Realizing that Hippomenes had taken the lead again, Atalanta took off running to catch up with him. This time it was a little more difficult for her. She was now carrying the heavier load as Hippomenes's load was getting lighter. She did, however, pass him and regained the lead.

As they drew closer to the finish line, Hippomenes reached into his tunic and took out the last golden apple, hoping Atalanta would be so focused on the attraction of the golden apples that she would lose the race. He tossed the last apple by Atalanta, only this time he tossed it even further off the path.

Hippomenes was right—the golden apples obsessed Atalanta. She now had a decision. Should she stay on the path or leave to get the last golden apple? She knew she was the faster runner and that she could probably get the third golden apple and still win the race. She decided to go for it. She left the path, quickly grabbed the apple, and again chased after Hippomenes.

Atalanta gained on Hippomenes as they approached the finish line, but she struggled because of the weight of the apples. Hippomenes, now free from any encumbrance, literally ran for his life.

Hippomenes did win the race. He won the beautiful Atalanta as his bride. And they lived happily ever after with their three golden apples.

"So, what's the point?" you ask.

You see, in the leadership race of life we have someone who is running behind us. He's the enemy of our souls. He doesn't want our hand in marriage. He simply wants us to detour off the straight and narrow path and lose the race. His strategy is to toss temptation alongside us so that we will become distracted from the goal of staying on the straight and narrow path and winning the race.

Shrewd, cunning, and clever, he first brings temptation very close to the path. He designs it in such a way that we don't stray far from the straight path...just a little way off. He knows he has future temptations that will get us to step further and further off the path until we lose the race. He wants us to lose our moral standing, our character, and our reputation. He knows the best way to accomplish this is to get our eyes on something that will distract us.

Hardly a month passes until we hear of someone in leadership failing morally. Everyone has temptations, but those in leadership seem to have a greater negative impact. Are there any shiny golden apples rolling near your path today? Or have you already stepped off the path and are chasing some golden apple to satisfy your desire? Those around you may not be aware that you've started to detour, but they'll soon find out. Now is the time to heed the warning signs. Think of all you're risking. Please turn back before it's too late.

> But remember this—the wrong desires that come into your life aren't anything new and different. Many others have faced exactly the same problems before you. And no temptation is irresistible. You can trust God to keep the temptation from becoming so strong that you can't stand up against it, for he has promised this and will do what he says. He will show you how to escape temptation's power so that you can bear up patiently against it (1 Corinthians 10:13 TLB).

> Since we have such a huge crowd of men of faith watching us from the grandstands, let us strip off anything that slows us down or holds us back, and especially those sins that wrap themselves so tightly around our feet and trip

us up; and let us run with patience the particular race that God has set before us (Hebrews 12:1 TLB).

I advise you to obey only the Holy Spirit's instructions. He will tell you where to go and what to do, and then you won't always be doing the wrong things your evil nature wants you to. For we naturally love to do evil things that are just the opposite from the things the Holy Spirit tells us to do; and the good things we want to do when the Spirit has his way with us are just the opposite of our natural desires. These two forces within us are constantly fighting each other to win control over us and our wishes are never free from their pressures...But when you follow your own wrong inclinations your lives will produce these evil results: impure thoughts, eagerness for lustful pleasure, idolatry, spiritism (that is, encouraging the activity of demons), hatred and fighting, jealousy and anger, constant effort to get the best for yourself, complaints and criticisms, the feeling that everyone else is wrong except those in your own little group—and there will be wrong doctrine, envy, murder, drunkenness, wild parties, and all that sort of thing. Let me tell you again as I have before, that anyone living that sort of life will not inherit the Kingdom of God (Galatians 5:16-17,19-21 TLB).

Dear Lord, ————————————————————————————

I need You to tap me on the shoulder when the golden apples of temptation are rolling about me. Help me to realize all that could be lost and the people who could be hurt, by my taking a detour from the straight and narrow path. Help me to read and memorize Bible verses, which can be claimed at the moment of temptation. Help me take responsibility and accountability for all my actions. Help me to change my thinking pattern, which wants to always justify my behavior. I want to be straightforward and honest in all that I do.

———————————————————————————— *Amen*

LEADERSHIP SUCCESS

A silly idea is current that good people do not know what temptation means. This is an obvious lie. Only those who try to resist temptation know how strong it is... A man who gives in to temptation after five minutes simply does not know what it would have been like an hour later. That is why bad people, in one sense, know very little about badness. They have lived a sheltered life by always giving in.

C.S. LEWIS

Free cheese is always available in mousetraps.
It's easier to avoid temptation than to resist it.
Opportunity may only knock once,
but temptation leans on the doorbell.

3

Managing Your Time

Time is an equal opportunity employer. Each human being has exactly the same number of hours and minutes every day. Rich people can't buy more hours. Scientists can't invent new minutes. You can't save time to spend it on another day. Even so, time is amazingly fair and forgiving. No matter how much time you've wasted in the past, you still have an entire tomorrow. Success depends upon using it wisely— by planning and setting priorities.

DENIS WAITLEY

How would you like to have three extra months a year? Would this help you get everything done? It's estimated that we spend up to six weeks a year looking for stuff. Imagine that—a month and a half! We could gain over a month's time just by getting organized. This is what Einstein meant when he said, "Out of clutter, find simplicity."

I don't have a count of the hours I've spent looking for things like my phone, glasses, and car keys. This does not include the wasted time trying to find something in my computer because I forgot how I titled it or which folder I put it in.

Clutter not only hides things, but it sucks creativity and energy from your brain. What are the ramifications of getting organized? It means a few things must be thrown away. This will be hard for some individuals. Getting organized means turning off the television, not going golfing, and not shopping. It means cleaning out the garage, organizing a closet, and straightening the drawer by the telephone. And it means throwing away magazines, junk mail, and outdated and underused possessions. The process of throwing away things can be softened by having a garage sale. You may even earn a little money for your effort. Or you could give items to the Salvation Army or your favorite charity.

Organizing starts by creating files for things you would like to keep. This includes important information that needs to be read or kept for future retrieval. This important information does not include hate mail you have received over the years. Burn those items just as Cortez burned his ships. No turning back. You don't need those reminders.

You will also have to learn to say no. This means you might need to resign from some committees or boards. It means some people may be upset with you because you are not doing what they would like you to do. You might even have to regain control if your schedule is too busy and stressful.

Several years ago I attended a conference for counselors. While there I met another counselor, and we shared about our counseling practices. After a period of time, the man looked at me and said, "I think you are a pretty good counselor. How long are you going to last?" His words haunted me. He had a good point because I was burning the candle at both ends. I realized that it was survival time for me, and I wanted to be a counselor for the long haul. I went home and reorganized my life. I cut my schedule back and began to say no.

Getting organized allows you freedom and control. It helps you avoid conflicts and guilt and the need to perform. It might even give you extra time to relax.

I haven't forgotten about the other two months I mentioned earlier. You can gain them by getting up one hour earlier each day. This will give you 365 extra hours. Divide that by eight working hours a day times five days, times four weeks a month, and you come up with more than two extra months a year to accomplish some of the things you would like to do.

This will give you time to exercise each day or meditate more or increase your reading time. It will give you time to study if you are going back to school or want to update your skills. You may even wish to spend some time exploring your spiritual gifts.

Therefore see that you walk carefully [living life with honor, purpose, and courage; shunning those who tolerate and enable evil], not as the unwise, but as wise [sensible, intelligent, discerning people], making the very most of your time [on earth, recognizing and taking advantage of each opportunity and using it with wisdom and diligence], because the days are [filled with] evil (Ephesians 5:15-16).

Dear Lord,

Please help me take a hard look at my life and what I've been doing. I need to develop some goals—not just little ones, but long-term ones. Help me stretch in this area. Please give me some new thoughts about what You think I should be doing. Help me stop procrastinating, get organized, and throw away all the clutter in my life. I have wasted much valuable time that is lost forever. Help me schedule myself better. Help me to be a leader that can be an example of positive organization. Help me to use my time wisely.

Amen

LEADERSHIP SUCCESS

It must be borne in mind that the tragedy of life doesn't lie in not reaching your goal. The tragedy lies in having no goal to reach. It isn't a calamity to die with dreams unfilled, but it is a calamity not to dream. It is not a disgrace not to reach the stars, but it is a disgrace to have no stars to reach for. Not failure, but low aim, is a sin.

~ BENJAMIN E. MAYS

4

Moving On: The Practice of Forgiveness

*Everyone says forgiveness is a lovely idea,
until they have something to forgive.*

C.S. Lewis

Have you ever wondered why forgiveness is so difficult? It's because the injured party lets the person who has done the injury go free. Archibald Hart says it this way; "Forgiveness is surrendering my right to hurt you back if you hurt me." Mark Twain expressed the same concept when he stated, "Forgiveness is the fragrance the violet sheds on the heel that has crushed it."

Imagine that I come over to your house to visit. You invite me in, and we go into your living room. You say, "Please sit down." For some reason I choose not to sit in a big soft chair but instead sit down in a small rocking chair. Before you can speak, the small rocking chair collapses under my weight. You see, I didn't know it was an antique rocking chair that been handed down through your family. To you it was a "display piece" in your home. Everyone is in shock.

I say, "I'm sorry. Can I buy you a new one?"

"No," you reply.

"Can I replace it?"

"No," you say with sadness in your voice.

"Will you forgive me?"

Inside, you groan with pain.

Can you see why forgiveness is so difficult? The person who inflicts the injury goes free, leaving the injured party in pain and misery. This is a dirty, unfair deal. It's not a pleasant experience in the least. *Repayment* for the offense is impossible. I cannot put the broken chair back into the same condition it was before the accident. Your trying to get *revenge* on me would not replace the chair. *Resenting* me for breaking the chair would not restore it. In forgiveness the injured party must make peace with the pain and accept the loss. This is why most people do not like to forgive—it's too painful and too costly.

> The weak can never forgive;
> forgiveness is the attribute of the strong.
>
> ~ Mahatma Gandhi

Forgiveness is found in the will. It's a promise—a commitment to three things, as Jay E. Adams suggests:

1. I will not use the event against them in the future.

2. I will not talk to others about them.

3. I will not dwell on it myself.

Forgiveness does not beat the offending party over the head with their offense, trying to make them feel guilty. It does not try to destroy the reputation of the offending party or get revenge by sharing the transgression with others. Forgiveness does not wallow in the misery of the conflict. It gets up and moves on with life. It does not rip off the scabs to see if the offense is healing, because this only prolongs the hurt.

> There is no point in burying the hatchet
> if you're going to put up a marker on the site.
>
> ~ Sydney Harris

What is the purpose of forgiveness? The act of forgiveness restores and reconciles broken relationships. What happens if one of the parties does not want to restore the relationship? Does forgiveness still take place? That's like asking, "Which came first, the chicken or the egg?" Does forgiveness take place first and then repentance, or does repentance take place first and then forgiveness?

To answer the first question—the chicken comes first. God does not lay any eggs. To answer the second question—forgiven. first, then repentance. Christ is our example in this. He forgives u. our sins before we repent.

The joy that forgiveness brings comes when we repent and turn from our sin. We can forgive others their offenses, but we both may not experience the joy of restoration and reconciliation until the offender repents. Sometimes they do not repent, and we are left with true but hollow forgiveness. That's a painful experience.

When you forgive someone and he or she does not repent, it hurts. In a very small way, you experience how God feels when people will not turn from their sins and accept His forgiveness. The heart of God aches because of His love for them. He does not turn His back on them because of their rejection. He keeps reaching out with the desire that someday they will repent and run back into His arms. We should follow His example.

> One pardons to the degree that one loves.
>
> ~ Francois de La Rochefoucauld

Part of your success as a leader is to provide an example of forgiveness. This is also your responsibility. Forgiveness is commanded by God as an act of how we should live in harmony with others. It was illustrated when Christ died for our sins and let us go free:

> So, as those who have been chosen of God, holy and beloved, put on a heart of compassion, kindness, humility, gentleness and patience; bearing with one another, and forgiving each other, whoever has a complaint against anyone; just as the Lord forgave you, so also should you (Colossians 3:12-13 NASB).

Dear Lord, ─────────────────────────

This is a hard one. I've struggled with forgiving some people for what they have said and done to me. I've been wallowing in the muddy swamp of resentment, and I don't have a lot of energy to climb out. I have tried before, but I keep sliding back in. Please send a rescue team immediately! Also send a big water truck of forgiveness to wash away the pain and self-pity that has covered my life. I would like to get cleaned up so that I can be used by You to help others who are also in the swamp of unforgiveness. I want to experience the joy of reconciliation with You and with those whom I have been resenting. I want to be a forgiving leader.

Amen

LEADERSHIP SUCCESS

Sometimes we find it hard to forgive. We forget that forgiveness is as much for us as for the other person. If you can't forgive it's like holding a hot coal in your hand—you're the one getting burned.

~ JENNIFER JAMES

5

Earning Trust: The Practice of Integrity

Integrity is the first button on the shirt of character.
If you get that button right,
the rest of the character buttons will fall into place.

Where does the word *integrity* come from? It comes from the Greek words *integritas* and *integra*. These words carry the concepts of wholeness, completeness, and soundness. In mathematics we have the word *integer*, which refers to whole numbers rather than fractions or divided numbers.

A person with integrity is straightforward, consistent, and honest. They are not corrupted, divided, or dishonest in their morality. Their actions are consistent and match their stated beliefs. They "talk the walk and walk the talk." They are trustworthy in their dealings with others. The person with integrity is truthful, dependable, and sincere. They are free of deceit, falseness, or hypocrisy.

Our first President of the United States, George Washington, once stated, "I hope I shall always possess firmness and virtue enough to maintain what I consider the most enviable of all titles, the character of an 'honest man.'"

Do you remember the fable Aesop told of the little boy who cried wolf? He was a lonely shepherd boy who wanted someone to talk with, but no one was around. He thought of a plan to get people interested in him and to come visit him. He began to scream and cry, "Wolf, wolf, wolf!" The people of the village heard his cry for help and came to rescue him and his sheep from the attack of a wolf. But as you recall there was no wolf. The people were upset with his dishonesty and went back to the village, leaving him all alone.

You will recall that he did the same thing on two more occasions when there was no wolf. Finally, one day a real wolf did attack the sheep, and the boy cried, "Wolf, wolf, wolf!" but no one came to his aid. Because of his lying and dishonesty, he had lost all reputation for integrity.

People do not want to follow a leader that is dishonest and untrustworthy. The leader without integrity becomes the hypocrite wearing the two-faced mask.

In our courts of law, we are told to *"Tell the truth"* (not to deceive with falsehood), *"the whole truth"* (not to leave any details out of the story), and *"nothing but the truth"* (not to add details to confuse or mislead the hearers).

I'm reminded of the story Charles Swindoll told about the man visiting a Kentucky Fried Chicken restaurant. He and his female friend went into the restaurant and ordered some take-out food. They wanted to have a short picnic in a nearby park.

They got their order and went to the park. Upon arriving they noticed something wrong with their order. As they opened the box that was to contain their chicken, they were shocked. Instead of chicken, the box was filled with money.

They went back to the restaurant and asked to see the manager. As the manager came toward the counter, he noticed the couple with their take-out sack. He assumed something was wrong.

"May I help you?" he asked.

"Yes, there is something wrong with our order."

When the manager opened the box and noticed the money, he almost collapsed.

It seems that he had cleaned out all the extra cash from the registers and put the money in a chicken box. His plan was to take the box back to his office and count the money. However, one of the employees distracted him and asked him a question. One of the other employees thought that box was part of the couple's order and put it in their carryout sack by mistake.

"Thank you for being so honest to bring the money back," said the manager. "Not many people have honesty and integrity like you have."

The manager then asked the man to please stay there while he called the local newspaper to send over a reporter to write up the story about the returned money.

The man told the manager that writing the story would not be necessary. The manager then tried again to get him to stay and write up the story. The man said, "Thank you, but we need to go."

The manager insisted one more time.

Finally the man responded, "You don't seem to understand. The woman I'm with is not my wife."

How are you doing in the area of integrity? Are you an honest person? Can people trust you? Are you an authentic person of your word? Do you tell the truth? Do you need to work on telling the truth, the whole truth, and nothing but the truth?

> He who walks in integrity and with moral character walks securely, but he who takes a crooked way will be discovered and punished...The integrity and moral courage of the upright will guide them, but the crookedness of the treacherous will destroy them...Better is the poor who walks in his integrity than he who is crooked and two-faced though he is rich (Proverbs 10:9; 11:3; 28:6).

Dear Lord,

Help me to realize the importance of honesty and integrity. Help me to become truthful in all my statements. Help me not to leave out facts that are important and help me not to add statements that are meant to confuse or hide information when I talk with family, friends, and fellow workers. I want people to be able to trust my words and actions. By Your Holy Spirit convict me of areas that need to be changed or cleaned up. I want my speech to be straightforward and pure. Help me to be more like You in holiness and godliness.

Amen

LEADERSHIP SUCCESS

Leadership is a potent combination of strategy and character
But if you must be without one, be without strategy.

NORMAN SCHWARZKOPF

6

Courage

We are face to face with our destiny,
and we must meet it with a high and resolute courage.
For us is the life of action, of strenuous performance of duty;
let us live in the harness, striving mightily;
let us rather run the risk of wearing out than rusting out.

~ THEODORE ROOSEVELT

Life does not compensate us for insight, understanding, wisdom, or intention. It only rewards action. I can tell the Internal Revenue Service that I intended to pay my taxes, but all they care about is the money. I can tell my wife that I understand how tired she is, but she would appreciate more my doing the dishes. I can tell my mechanic that I have gained much insight as to how the internal combustion engine runs, but all he will ask is, "Did you put oil in it?" I can tell my children that I read a book and acquired greater wisdom on being a father, but all they care about is if I attended their soccer game. Henry Ford said, "You can't build a reputation on what you intend to do." It's so easy to get wrapped up in mind games and forget practical, daily living.

How do you begin to deal with your problems? Some schools of thought would say, "We need to find the root of the problem. We need to dredge through the garbage dump of our past and find the original causes to what's bothering us now."

I realize that some insight and important information can be gained by searching through the past. However, the more important issue is what is presently going on in your life and what you want to change for the future.

Let's say that you and I were in the mountains admiring the beautiful rocks and trees. All of a sudden, we hear a noise and look up. It's the sound of an avalanche. Huge boulders are rolling down the mountain toward us. We are standing in the pathway and will most likely soon be crushed to death.

With a frightened look you turn to me. I respond by saying, "Be calm. All we have to do is to find out what started the avalanche, and we will be safe. We need to find the root cause for why those rocks started rolling toward us."

You reply, "You're out of your mind! What we need to do is start running for our lives from the biggest boulders!"

You would be absolutely correct. It is only after we are safe from the biggest boulders that we can take the time to determine how it all got started. And maybe then, when we are safe from the biggest boulders, it wouldn't even matter how they all got started. Probably a more important issue would be how to escape from boulders in the future and how not to get any more rolling.

What are the big boulders in your life? Are you scared enough to run for your life? Have you been "hurt" enough to change?

I remember talking to one individual about a pressing situation in his life. I listened to his story for a while and then said, "I don't think you've hurt enough yet." I could see the look of shock on his face. *Of course I'm hurting,* he thought. I went on to say, "When you hurt enough, you will change."

Let's say you and I were standing in a parking lot talking. During our conversation, I hit you on your shoulder. The punch caught you off guard. *What is he doing?* you think. Our talk continues, and I hit you again. You think, *How dare he hit me. Who does he think he is?* It isn't long before I hit you again. This time you back away from me. We keep on talking, and I hit you a fourth time.

How many hits would you take before you would say to me, "Knock it off!" The truth of the matter is, you would tell me to stop when you got sick and tired of me hitting you.

Are you sick and tired of taking emotional hits in your life? When you become tired enough...you will change. If you're not quite to that place yet, it's okay. You're in the process. You just need to hurt a little more because *people only change when they hurt enough.*

I'm reminded of the story of the young man who wanted to become very wise. He traveled all over the world talking with people. One day he heard there was an extremely wise man who lived in the mountains of Mexico.

After many days of travel, the young man came upon the house of the wise man. The young man knocked, and the old man opened the door. The young man introduced himself and asked the old man if he was the wise man he was looking for. The old man carefully looked at the young man and said, "Perhaps."

For several days the young man told his story of his search for wisdom. The old man listened quietly. Finally the young man ran out of words and said, "Do you have any wise thoughts for me?"

The old man said, "Perhaps." He then motioned for the young man to follow him. They walked down a path toward a beautiful lake.

Upon arriving the young man said, "This is breathtaking. Is this where I can obtain wisdom?"

"Perhaps," said the old man.

The old man took the young man to the side of the lake and said, "Bend over and look carefully into the dark water." The young man got on his knees, bent over, and peered into the water. He could see his own face in the reflection of the still water.

Suddenly, the old man pushed the young man's head under water. He struggled to break free but could not because the old man was very strong. Soon he could feel himself starting to lose consciousness from the lack of air.

At that point, the old man pulled the young man's head out of the water. The young man gasped for air and yelled, "What are you doing? You almost killed me! You're crazy!"

"Perhaps," said the old man. "But when you truly search for wisdom and want to change as much as you were fighting for air, then you will become wise."

My dear reader, when you seek emotional health and freedom from your hurt and pain as much as you would fight for air—when you take action and yell, "Knock it off!"—then you, too, will change.

> Don't be misled; remember that you can't ignore God and get away with it: a man will always reap just the kind of crop he sows! If he sows to please his own wrong desires, he will be planting seeds of evil and he will surely reap a harvest of spiritual decay and death; but if he plants the good things of the Spirit, he will reap everlasting life that the Holy Spirit gives him (Galatians 6:7-8 TLB).

Dear Lord,

I am the King (Queen) of excuses and rationalizations. I've tried all of them, but none of them brought happiness. I've been sowing an unsuccessful pile of seeds. I'm tired of all the pain, hurt, and suffering I've been feeling. I know I can't make the changes by myself. I've tried time and again, and it only ends in failure. Please help me to act on the areas in my life that need to change. I've come to the end of my resources like the prodigal son when he ran away from home. I'm tired of the emotional "pig pen" I've been wallowing in. It's time for me to take action and get my head out of the dark water and get on with life. I'm reaching my hand out to You for assistance.

Amen

LEADERSHIP SUCCESS

All the good maxims have been written. It only remains to put them into practice.

~ BLAISE PASCAL

7

Accountability

When two men ride a horse, one must ride behind.

t was a bad day for Cory Wagner. He was upset and frustrated with his boss Matt Whitmeyer who had just held a sales meeting in the conference room. Cory thought Matt was incompetent, wouldn't listen to others, and was a poor decision maker. Cory's body language was easy to read as he shook his head back and forth and expelled loud sighs.

Cory had been promoted from salesman to become the manager of the sales department for the Craigmore Corporation. He had been in that position for about a year. He was standing at the water cooler when Ben Setter walked by and noticed him.

Ben was one of Craigmore's top salesmen. He had been with the company for 20 years and was nearing retirement. He had been in the same meeting with Cory, Matt, and other sales people.

"You seem upset, Cory," said Ben.

"Whitmeyer is an idiot. I don't know how he ever got the job as CEO."

"Let's go to my office and talk for a few minutes," said Ben.

"That will probably be helpful," replied Cory.

After Cory calmed a little, Ben asked, "Cory, who is the CEO for Craigmore?"

With a quizzing look he said, "Matt Whitmeyer."

"At the sales meeting, did Matt suggest we do anything illegal, unlawful, or immoral?"

"No, he didn't."

"But you have strong disagreements with him, don't you?"

"I sure do. I still think he's an idiot."

Ben pressed a little further. "What did you specifically disagree with? Territorial space, schedules, methods, or procedures? Or was it the conflict over personal preferences, traditions, customs, values, or beliefs?"

"What are you trying to say, Ben?"

"I guess I'm saying that Matt's the boss and you're not. He didn't ask you to do anything illegal, unlawful, or immoral. He didn't choose to go your direction, and now you're mad and upset. I think you would be wiser to do what he asked you to do."

"But what if he's wrong. What then?"

"Then the authority, the decision, and the responsibility reside with Matt. He becomes accountable. It sounds like you are vying for control and want to be the boss. Is that possible?"

Cory was quiet, considering what Ben said.

Ben continued, "Cory, if you have a disagreement or concern about something, let me suggest a more tactful way to go about it. Approach Matt when no one else is around. Ask him if he has a few minutes to talk about a matter. When he's available to talk, the next statement is very important. Begin the talk and concern by asking, 'Sir, do I have permission to speak frankly?' When he says yes, share your thoughts without a lot of emotion. Stick to the facts and concerns, and then hear him out."

Cory was listening carefully to Ben's wise advice.

"Now, Matt may not agree with you, or he may agree with your suggestions. Either way you have his attention and he is now aware of your thoughts. Remember, Matt does not work for you. You work for him and you need to be grateful that you have a job. Many people do not have work to pay their bills."

> Sometimes the kindest thing you can do for a person
> is to tell him a truth that will prove very painful.
> But in so doing, you may have saved him
> from serious harm or even greater pain. In a world such as ours,
> people must learn to "take it." A painless world
> is not necessarily a good world.
>
> ~ SYLVANUS AND EVELYN DUVALL

Ben went on, "Cory, psychologists tell us there are three major reasons we criticize other people. The first is we are guilty of doing the same thing. Second, we are miserable and want to project our own miserableness. It's been said that misery loves company. We love to get people on our side. And the third reason is that we criticize others in order to elevate ourselves and to put others down. Do any of those reasons ring a bell for you?"

Cory's head bent a little lower as he listened to Ben.

"One other thought. When we put down our boss in the eyes of others...and when we openly disagree with our boss...and when we disobey their direction or orders, we train others who work for us to do the same thing to us. They will disagree with and disobey your orders. Cory, one of the secrets to leadership success is loyalty to the legitimate authority over us...even if we do not always agree with them."

Cory sheepishly lifted his head and nodded. "I guess I have some growing up to do."

> Show respect for all people [treat them honorably], love the brotherhood [of believers], fear God, honor the king.
>
> Servants, be submissive to your masters with all [proper] respect, not only to those who are good and kind, but also to those who are unreasonable (1 Peter 2:17-18).

Dear Lord,

It's so easy to follow in the footsteps of Cory and criticize, gripe, and complain about those in authority above us. I've been guilty of doing the very same thing in the past. Help me to grow up and face conflict and disagreement as an adult. Remind me to approach those over me with honor and respect. Help me to be grateful for having the privilege to have a job and contribute to society. Give me the courage to lead others with a Christlike example of humility and openness.

Amen

LEADERSHIP SUCCESS

When a gentleman hath learned to obey, he will grow very much fitter to command; his own memory will advise him not to command too rigorous punishments.

~ LORD HALIFAX

8

Taking Action

*If you really want to do something, you'll find a way—
if not, you'll find an excuse.*

~Jim Rohn

Thinking about doing something is not the same thing as doing it. Thinking about stealing is not stealing. Thinking about dishonesty is not the same as lying. One can lead to the other, but they're not the same. You can say both are wrong (and they are), but thinking about breaking something is not the same as doing it.

Often people think about doing the right thing. They dwell on those thoughts and evaluate just the best way to do the right thing—but they never act! I call this "Aristotelian" logic. Aristotle used a train of thought called *deductive* logic and reasoning to come to his conclusions. This is the process of creating propositions in terms of their forms (abstract or general) instead of their content (actual and specific).

Our society is filled with Aristotelian logic. For example, would you like to be able to play the piano? I mean just sit down and play almost any tune that comes to your mind. Wouldn't it be fun to be the life of the party and lead others in group singing or maybe even play in a concert? Possibly you would prefer to quietly play for yourself for sheer enjoyment. You might even entertain the thought of creating your own songs for others to enjoy. Wouldn't that be a wonderful talent to have?

I'm sure there would be a host of people who would raise their hands and say, "I'd like to be able to play the piano. It would be fun. I would really like to do it." That's an example of Aristotelian logic. It has become a little warped from Aristotle's original intention, but it's part of the fabric of American society and thinking. In a nutshell it says, "Since I *think* I would like to play the piano, and since I *feel* like I would like the piano, it's true. It's *reality* for me. Conclusion: I would like to play the piano."

This deductive reasoning is the belief that if I repeat something often enough, it will become true in my mind. That's why some people who exaggerate and lie long enough begin to believe their own falsehoods as truth.

There's another form of thinking that I call "Hebraic" logic. Rather than using deduction, starting at the beginning, and coming to a conclusion, this method uses the train of thought called *induction*. It looks at a specific or particular thought or activity and then begins to make a general conclusion.

Let's go back to the piano. The individual using Hebraic logic would ask, "Do you practice and play the piano?" (specific and pointed). "No, but I would like to" (general and abstract). At which point the person using Hebraic logic would say, "No, you really would not like to play. For if you really wanted to play the piano, you would do so. You would put forth the effort to practice. As a result of your practice, you would play the piano." Conclusion: You don't really want to play, or you would play.

Hebraic logic basically says, "Actions speak louder than words. What you are speaks so loudly that I can't hear what you are saying. Don't talk the walk if you don't walk the talk." Ralph Waldo Emerson said, "Thought is the blossom; language the bud; action the fruit behind it."

Listed below are a few quotes concerning a train of thought that's action-orientated.

> Do you want to know who you are? Don't ask. Act!
> Action will delineate and define you.
>
> ~ THOMAS JEFFERSON

> An inch of movement will bring you closer
> to your goal than a mile of intention.
>
> ~ STEVE MARABOLI

Characterize people by their actions
and you will never be fooled by their words.
Actions prove who someone is,
words just prove who they want to be.
You are what you do,
not what you say you'll do.

~ Carl Jung

When your actions contradict your words,
your words don't mean anything.
People judge you by your actions
not your intentions.
You don't have to be great to start
but you have to start to be great.

~ Zig Zigler

The very word *leader* carries the concept of action, movement, and direction. How are you doing in this area? Is your day filled with intention or action? We're not talking about fruitless and pointless action and movement. We're talking about action and leadership that's moving toward a positive and worthwhile goal. As a leader they do not pay you to just sit there and come up with intention. They're paying you to produce and accomplish. Enough talk. It's time to "get-'er-done."

But prove yourselves doers of the word [actively and continually obeying God's precepts], and not merely listeners [who hear the word but fail to internalize its meaning], deluding yourselves [by unsound reasoning contrary to the truth]. For if anyone only listens to the word without obeying it, he is like a man who looks very carefully at his natural face in a mirror; for *once* he has looked at himself and gone away, he immediately forgets what he looked like. But he who looks carefully into the perfect law, the *law* of liberty, and faithfully abides by it, not having become a [careless] listener who forgets but an active doer [who obeys], he will be blessed *and* favored by God in what he does [in his life of obedience]...But someone may say, "You [claim to] have faith and I have [good] works; show me your [alleged] faith without the works [if you can], and I will show you my faith by my works [that is, by what I do]" (James 1:22-25; 2:18).

Dear Lord,

Help me to utilize more Hebraic thinking in my leadership. Lead me and teach me how to move from necessary intention to practical action. I know it's my responsibility to lead those under my supervision. Help me not only to be accountable to those who employ me but also to those who look to me for leadership. Guide me, and guard me from pathways that could lead in a direction that would be detrimental to my family, those I work with, and the organization I serve. I want to become a doer of Your Word.

Amen

LEADERSHIP SUCCESS

Action is the foundational key to all success.

~ PABLO PICASSO

9

Leadership Starts at Home

*It is my view that our society can be no more stable than the
foundation of individual family units upon which it rests.
Our government, our institutions, our schools...indeed,
our way of life are dependent on healthy marriages
and loyalty to the vulnerable little children around our feet.*

~ JAMES DOBSON

Leadership in the home affects all areas of society. A happy marriage helps to create a stable home filled with peace and tranquility. Unfortunately, not all marriages are happy and secure. Many marriages experience turmoil and disruption.

What should you do when you encounter a marriage that's dysfunctional and turbulent? It's essential to discover those factors that tend to destroy a marriage and what you can do to put the marriage back on track.

As a marriage counselor I've had the privilege of officiating weddings for a number of couples. That's great and wonderful on the positive side. On the negative side I've also had the opportunity to assist couples to renew and restore marriages that were heading toward divorce—not always an easy task.

In all my years of counseling, I've never had someone come into my office and say, "My spouse is so kind, loving, and generous. They are so attentive and encouraging to me that I want a divorce. They are so good and forgiving that I want out of this marriage." That would be a first. You see, two unselfish people never get a divorce.

Many factors lead to divorce, but it basically boils down to this: People have an opportunity to do a loving activity for their mate, and they choose not to do it. That choosing *not to do* loving activities begins to build up until there is a whole pile or collection of hurts and disappointments. Finally, one or both marriage partners says, "I don't feel like I love them anymore!"

When the couple comes into my office, I don't delve into trying to find out all the reasons why they don't love each other anymore. Those are their feelings at that time. I simply look at them and ask, "Would you like to feel like you loved them again?" This startles them a little because they're not sure if that is even possible with all the hurt they have experienced.

I then suggest that five things *when done* will put their marriage back together again.

1. It begins with saying, **"*I'm sorry.*"** That's the starting place. The great preacher Charles Hadden Spurgeon said, "Sorrow pays no debt." For example, if I accidently break an antique vase while visiting your home, my first response would be, "I'm sorry. Can I buy you another one?"
   "No," you respond.
   "Can I pay you what it's worth?"
   "No, it's priceless to me."
   The person who is injured pays the price for the injury, and the guilty party goes free. Now that's a dirty deal isn't it?
   What then does sorrow do? It says to the other party, "I realize that I've hurt you, and I'm taking ownership and responsibility for my part in the hurt."

2. The next thing to say is, **"*I've been wrong.*"** This takes sorrow to the next level in the form of repenting for the hurt caused. It conveys the concept of wanting to make an about-face from wrong to right, and not to commit the wrong again. It's extremely humbling to admit you are wrong and want to change. Some people struggle with this second step because they've been selfish for a long period of time. It's hard to eat crow regardless if it is baked, stewed, or fried. Just saying those words in your mind is difficult to admit.

3. The third thing to say is, **"*Please forgive me.*"** The guilty party is now at the mercy of the person they have hurt. The hurt partner could say, "Yes, I'll forgive you," or they could say, "No, I'll not forgive you." Again, this is a very difficult position for the injured party.

4. The next thing to say is, **"*I love you.*"** This is a recommitment of your heart, mind, and desire. Those three words are a reaching out to the one who has been hurt with the reassurance that you are still there with no intent to leave the relationship.

5. The last thing to express is the sentence, **"*Let's try again.*"** It's like taking a wet sponge and wiping clean a slate or chalkboard of all the past chalk marks. It's not bringing up the past to use it against the partner anymore. It's not talking to others about all the spouse's misdeeds. It's a choice not to dwell on past hurts in your mind.

Now what? Now you start again doing loving activities one after another as proof that you were serious. Proof that you want to be a leader in your own home.

> Be gentle and forbearing with one another and, if one has a difference (a grievance or complaint) against another, readily pardoning each other; even as the Lord has [freely] forgiven you, so must you also [forgive]. And above all these [put on] love *and* enfold yourselves with the bond of

perfectness [which binds everything together completely in ideal harmony]. And let the peace (soul harmony which comes) from the Christ rule (act as umpire continually) in your hearts [deciding and settling with finality all questions that arise in your minds, in that peaceful state] to which as [members of Christ's] one body you were also called [to live]. And be thankful (appreciative), [giving praise to God always] (Colossians 3:13-15 AMPC).

Dear Lord,

Touch my mind and heart and remind me of how I may have hurt my spouse. Please point out those things I need to say I'm sorry for. Help me admit to my spouse where I have been wrong in what I have said and wrong in my attitude toward them. Humble me to ask for forgiveness. Help me to reinforce my love for them. Help me to be the leader in my home that I need to be. Give me a kick in the seat of the pants to start doing loving activities that I should be doing. Give me the courage to start today.

Amen

LEADERSHIP SUCCESS

Most arguments or conflicts tend to go downhill after 9:00 p.m. Hello. Start your discussions earlier. Go for a walk and talk. Most arguments in the family start half an hour before everyone goes to work or school or the half hour just before dinner when everyone is tired and frustrated from the day. Work on your timing. Most friction in life is caused by the tone of voice—or the misunderstanding of the tone of voice. Often the difference between a successful marriage and a mediocre one consists of leaving about three or four things a day unsaid. A successful marriage is an edifice that must be rebuilt every day.

10

The Power of Faith

We must never put our dreams of success as God's purpose for us;
His purpose may be exactly the opposite. His purpose is that
I depend on Him and in His power now. His end is the
process. It is the process, not the end, which is glorifying to
God...His purpose is for this minute, not for something in
the future. We have nothing to do with the "afterwards" of
obedience. If we have a further end in view, we do not pay
sufficient attention to the immediate present; if we realize that
obedience is the end, then each moment as it comes is precious.

~ OSWALD CHAMBERS

Electrical power is a form of energy. Without this energy engines would cease to run. Lights would go out. Heat would begin to diminish. Our television sets would grow dark. Our phones would not work. Our cars would not start. And there would be no Facebook or Twitter to occupy our time. No one would be texting us what they ate for lunch. Of course the last one would be a blessing rather than a curse.

When it comes to the area of leadership it, too, is a form of energy. The source of this energy must be generated from someplace. Usually it's generated within the heart and mind of the individual but influenced by primarily three outside sources: 1) Observing and being under various forms of leadership. 2) By reading authors about leadership. 3) By listening to speakers who instruct in the concepts of leadership. It's from these three sources that we begin to formulate our concept of leadership.

The *Powerhouse* source for leadership is found in the Bible. Not only does it make powerful suggestions that will enhance leadership, but it also gives us examples of both good and bad leadership.

I don't know where you stand regarding your view of God and the Bible. I can only share with you a wonderful truth I have found beneficial in my various leadership roles. As a man of faith, I believe that a Creator God exists. He knows and has created all the skills and techniques needed for effective leadership. He hasn't kept them to Himself. He has conveyed them within the covers of His Word, the Bible.

God wants us to become effective leaders for Him. This begins as we have a personal encounter with Him, as outlined in the book of Romans 10:9-11:

> Because if you acknowledge *and* confess with your mouth that Jesus is Lord [recognizing His power, authority, and majesty as God], and believe in your heart that God raised Him from the dead, you will be saved. For with the heart a person believes [in Christ as Savior] resulting in his justification [that is, being made righteous—being freed of the guilt of sin and made acceptable to God]; and with the mouth he acknowledges *and* confesses [his faith openly], resulting in *and* confirming [his] salvation. For the Scripture says, "Whoever believes in Him [whoever adheres to, trusts in, and relies on Him] will not be disappointed [in his expectations]."

This establishes a relationship with God and opens the floodgate of energy from His powerhouse to us. We can now draw on His principles for godly leadership. As you begin to study the Bible, God will reveal to you how you should act in leading, whether it's in your own family, your business, your community, or other service opportunities.

Many people do not know where to begin when studying the Bible. I would like to suggest one method of study for you to consider. It's called The Powerhouse Bible Study Plan. It's not complex at all. In fact, it's quite simple.

Open your Bible to any of the 66 individual books. They are listed in the table of contents in the beginning of your Bible. Select a book to read. I suggest you begin with the book of John in the New Testament. Plan to read one chapter a day. As you read the chapter, you are to look for the following things.

Look for God's commands. A command is something you are instructed to do. On a separate piece of paper write down the commands you find, and then attempt to follow through with them.

Look for God's promises. A promise is something God asks you to believe. Write down any promises you find. Then begin to practice believing them.

Look for the key verse. Find a verse you think summarizes the thoughts or stands out as very important. Write that verse down. You might even attempt to memorize it.

Look for any personal applications. When you find a verse or a thought that personally applies to your life or some situation you are facing, write it down. Ask yourself, *How can I apply this thought to my life today?* Then pray and ask God to help you apply that concept. Also ask Him to bring to mind throughout the day any of the commands or promises you found.

Plan to put into practice every day The Powerhouse Bible Study Plan. It's only one chapter a day. If you do this, you will begin to draw on God's wisdom for you and your leadership responsibilities.

> Like newborn babies [you should] long for the pure milk of the word, so that by it you may be nurtured *and* grow in respect to salvation [its ultimate fulfillment], if in fact you have [already] tasted the goodness and gracious kindness of the Lord (1 Peter 2:2-3).

> How can a young man keep his way pure? By keeping watch [on himself] according to Your word [conforming his life to Your precepts]. With all my heart I have sought You, [inquiring of You and longing for You] (Psalm 119:9-10).

Dear Lord, ————————————————————

I want to confess and acknowledge You as my Savior and Lord. I believe You died for my sins. I believe that You were raised from the dead as victory over sin and death. I desire to live my life for You. I need Your help in becoming the leader I need to be in my family and in my place of work. Help me to study Your Word and please make Your thoughts clear to me by Your Holy Spirit. Help me not only to read the Bible but to put it into practice in my leadership responsibilities. I look forward to what You will be teaching me. Thank You for loving me even though I am often unlovable.

Amen

LEADERSHIP SUCCESS

I am profitably engaged in reading the Bible. Take all of this Book that you can by reason and the balance by faith, and you will live and die a better man. It is the best Book which God has given to man.

~ ABRAHAM LINCOLN

There are times when solitude is better than society, and silence is wiser than speech. We should be better Christians if we were more alone, waiting upon God, and gathering through meditation on His Word spiritual strength for labor in His service. We ought to muse upon the things of God, because we thus get the real nutriment out of them... Why is it that some Christians, although they hear many sermons, make but slow advances in the divine life? Because they neglect their closets, and do not thoughtfully meditate on God's Word. They love the wheat, but they do not grind it; they would have the corn, but they will not go forth into the fields to gather it; the fruit hangs upon the tree, but they will not pluck it; the water flows at their feet, but they will not stoop to drink it. From such folly deliver us, O Lord.

~ CHARLES H. SPURGEON

11

Creating Your Ideal Job

I have looked in the mirror every morning and asked myself:
"If today were the last day of my life, would I want to do
what I am about to do today?" And whenever the answer
has been "No" for too many days in a row,
I know I need to change something.

~ STEVE JOBS

What is the ideal job? The standard answer: The ideal job is something you love doing. But for many people they don't completely love everything about their present job. They must have a job—whether they love it or not—to pay their bills, to put food on the table, and to support their family.

The question arises, "How can I survive and be a successful leader until I find that ideal or perfect job for me?"

Many years ago I took a test that helped to clarify this question. We were given three sheets of paper. On the top of the first sheet we were to put the title *My Ideal Job*. We were asked to write down a dozen things we felt would make up our ideal job. This included things like "I want to work inside" or "I want to work outside" and "I want to work with people" or "I want to work alone."

On the second sheet of paper we were to put the title *My Present Job*. We were asked to write down a dozen tasks or responsibilities that our present job entailed.

We were then told to compare the two lists and determine the similarities or the wide gap between them. If we discovered a vast difference, it was suggested that we should plan to seek a new job that would be closer to our *Ideal Job*—if we wanted to be happy for the long term.

On the third sheet of paper we were to put the title *My Avocation*. An avocation is a subordinate occupation, profession, or vocation. It could take the form of a hobby or calling. It could be referred to as a diversion, a sideline, or a spare-time interest. We were asked to list a dozen possibilities.

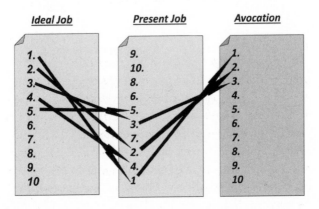

The test administrator suggested that if our *Present Job* gave us some of the items mentioned in our *Ideal Job*, we wouldn't necessarily have to leave our *Present Job*. We could supplement our desires by developing an *Avocation* outside of our *Present Job*. In this way we could have the best of two worlds.

In my case, my *Present Job* was to be the Executive Director of a large nonprofit youth camping program, which gave me much satisfaction. But I had a creative side not being fulfilled. I was hired to oversee a large ministry; they didn't hire me to write. I wanted to do some writing, so I developed an *Avocation* outside of my daily employment.

Where are you at this point? Are you in your *Ideal Job* now? Is there a wide difference between your *Ideal Job* and your *Present Job*? Then you may need to start thinking about a change. Or are you happy in your *Present Job* but need something more. It might be good for you to start thinking about an *Avocation*.

As a leader you might consider the needs of those working under you. They might be looking for their *Ideal Job*, and you could be used to help them to achieve their goal. Just a thought.

Well, one thing, at least, is good: It is for a man to eat well, drink a good glass of wine, accept his position in life, and enjoy his work whatever his job may be, for however long the Lord may let him live...The person who does that will not need to look back with sorrow on his past, for God gives him joy (Ecclesiastes 5:18-20 TLB).

Dear Lord,

I want to contribute and be happy in my work. I want to spend my lifetime and efforts in something I really enjoy. Please give me wisdom if I need to change my present job and find something more fulfilling. And if I'm to remain in my present job, help me to find ways to be happy and satisfied. Help me to be alert to others who may be struggling in this area and use me to encourage them. Lord, help me to consider an avocation that can expand my creative juices. I will be excited to see how You are going to lead me.

Amen

LEADERSHIP SUCCESS

It is the capacity to develop and improve their skills that distinguishes leaders from their followers.

~ WARREN BENNIS & BERT NANUS

DEALING WITH LEADERSHIP CHALLENGES

12

Dealing with Bad News

*Don't hide bad news. With multiple information channels available,
bad news always becomes known. Be candid right from the start.*

~ John C. Maxwell

Nathan was not looking forward to talking with his boss. The information he had to give was not positive. Making matters worse, his boss, Cal MacDonald, was known to have a short fuse and would get angry when his company wasn't running smoothly.

Nathan had been working in his position as finance manager for about two years. He had seen MacDonald's negative response to bad news during several company meetings. Now it was his turn to be the bearer of bad news. He had concerns that he, the messenger, might be attacked for sharing the message.

As a leader it's important you have enough information (facts and details) so you can make wise decisions for your business and for those who work for you. Those facts and details may not always be positive. Some of them might be negative and detrimental to you and your organization.

Information is like a traffic light with green, yellow, and red lights. The green light is good news. You can travel forward without hindrance or slowing down. The yellow light warns us that a change is coming, and we need to be alert to potential danger and slow down—don't speed up. The red light can be viewed as bad news because it hinders us and stops our forward motion. However, the red light can also be viewed as good news because our stopping could save our life from an accident or even death.

Good news and bad news are both only information. It's what you do with the information that's important. For you to make good decisions as the leader, you need to have both positive and negative facts and details. It has been said that a problem well-stated (facts and details) is a problem half-solved.

When it comes to bad news, we as leaders need to know the truth regardless of its ramifications. Abraham Lincoln stated, "Let the people know the truth and the country is safe."

How do you deal with bad news when you hear it? Do you get fearful or angry? Do you take out your frustration on those who bring you the information? Do you try to ignore the bad news and wish or pretend it doesn't exist? Or do you accept the bad news as simply more information that will help you to make good future decisions?

A friend of mine who was a police executive had 8,000 officers and 2,000 civilians working under his command. Charged with oversight for a large metropolitan city, he had many occasions to receive bad news. He didn't get upset with those who brought him bad news. The bad news aided him in making positive decisions as to where to deploy officers to deal with crime.

He became aware that some people were a little afraid to bring problems and bad news to him. They didn't want to add more bad news to the pile he was already dealing with. He then made a sign and put it up behind the chair in his office. Anyone coming into his office could see the sign behind him on the wall: BAD NEWS WELCOMED HERE!

When those working under you realize that you are open to hear not only good news but also bad news, they will become more confident in your leadership. They will realize it's important for you to have all the facts and details to be able to make good decisions. Their trust in your leadership will grow. How are you going to deal with bad news today?

Dear brothers, is your life full of difficulties and temptations? Then be happy, for when the way is rough, your patience has a chance to grow. So let it grow, and don't try to squirm out of your problems. For when your patience is finally in full bloom, then you will be ready for anything, strong in character, full and complete. If you want to know what God wants you to do, ask him, and he will gladly tell you, for he is always ready to give a bountiful supply of wisdom to all those ask him; he will not resent it (James 1:2-5 TLB)

Dear Lord,

You know I don't always relish bad news. It's not fun to think about. Yet I know this world is filled with both good and bad news. Help me to view news as information that I need so I can make good and effective decisions. Help me to view information as a traffic signal with green, yellow, and red lights. Please alert me not to make people who bring me bad news feel intimidated and anxious. Please help me to remember the sign over the police executive's desk that BAD NEWS IS WELCOMED HERE. Help me to live in the safety of truth.

Amen

LEADERSHIP SUCCESS

What separates slow, unproductive leaders from rapid, highly productive leaders is the ability to process information and make decisions.

13

Confronting Problems

When you confront a problem you begin to solve it.

~ RUDY GIULIANI

Derek was concerned, frustrated, and a little bit angry with Brent. Brent had been working for Derek for almost a year. He was an extremely hard-working employee who was always on time and willing to work extra hours if needed. Brent's attention to detail was above average, and he would accomplish tasks in a timely fashion. However, Brent had a problem. It was his mouth. On numerous occasions he would lose his temper and say harsh comments to other employees and sometimes customers.

Derek could not tolerate this type of behavior and knew he needed to confront Brent. Part of his concern was that he didn't want to confront in such a way as to lose a hard-working employee. He was also a little irritated that he had to take time out of his busy schedule to deal with this issue.

Derek wasn't quite sure how to approach the situation, but then he remembered a leadership seminar he had attended. The instructor had suggested a method of dealing with confrontation. He called it the Sandwich Technique.

The instructor went on to explain that a good way to deal with confrontation was to start out by saying something positive about the employee's performance, such as that he is a very hard-working employee. Follow up with a second positive statement to compliment the employee. For example: He spent important time accomplishing details.

At this point, the instructor suggested, the manager should "sandwich in" the negative behavior that needed to be confronted. After confronting the employee's actions and words (in this case, Brent's temper and harsh words), the leader should move to the next step of stating one or two more positive comments about the employee's performance.

> **One Positive Statement**
> **One Positive Statement**   *Sandwich*
> **One Negative Statement**   *Technique*
> **One or Two more Positive Statements**

Now, do you know the name of this sandwich? It is called a Baloney Sandwich. It doesn't work. You might ask, *Why?*

When you combine positive statements with negative statements, the person being confronted only hears and focuses on the negative statements. You've just thrown away three or four positive statements.

For example, if you're a husband: After your wife prepares a great meal for you, say to her, "Honey, that was a fantastic meal. It tasted wonderful. Tomorrow night I have a meeting and would appreciate it if you could get it on the table a little sooner so I won't be late for the meeting."

You have just given a positive and a negative statement together. Which one do you think your wife heard?

Or let's say you happen to run across an old friend that you haven't seen in several years. When you greet him you say, "Tom, it's been a long time. It's great to see you. Putting on a little weight I see." You have just given a positive and a negative statement together. Which one do you think Tom focused on...that you were happy to see him? I don't think so.

What's the point? There's a place for positive statements and there's a place for negative or confrontive statements. Don't throw away positive comments by combining negative comments with them.

Regarding Brent, it will be more beneficial to approach him directly concerning his inappropriate behavior. "Brent, are you aware of how you are coming across with other employees and customers? Your losing your temper and responding with harsh words cannot be tolerated." No mixed message or confusion is found in this approach.

Open rebuke is better than hidden love! Wounds from a friend are better than kisses from an enemy! (Proverbs 27:5-6 TLB).

Dear Lord,

Help me to be open, honest, and kind in all my relationships…even when I must confront someone about an issue. Help me to be an encourager and give positive messages at the appropriate times. And also help me to be lovingly confrontive when necessary. And, Lord, if I need to be confronted about some issue, help me to humbly accept the correction and make the necessary changes. Thank You for being so kind and loving to me when I don't even live up to the standards I hold for others. As I move into this day, help me to be alert to the needs of others.

Amen

LEADERSHIP SUCCESS

The challenge of leadership is to be strong, but not rude; be kind, but not weak; be bold, but not bully; be thoughtful, but not lazy; be humble, but not timid; be proud, but not arrogant; have humor, but without folly.

~ JIM ROHN

14

Overcoming Boredom

I am convinced that boredom is one of the greatest tortures.
If I were to imagine Hell, it would be the place
where you were continually bored.

~ Erich Fromm

D o you think it's possible for leaders to be bored? You already know
the answer to that question. It takes one to know one. The question really becomes, "Why do leaders get bored?"

I can think of several reasons. The first to come to mind is that the
leader is simply lazy and does not take responsibility for the role for
which they have been hired. They may not have anyone they answer
to, thus have no direct accountability to someone else or to a board of
directors. The old metaphor rings true: "When the cat's away the mice
will play." This type of leadership is corrupt.

Another reason could be the leader has a lack of skill or expertise
in a particular area. This lack of experience might cause them to avoid
or put off dealing with an important issue. Some leaders have a difficult time with creativity and vision casting. Others find that continually dealing with people is tremendously draining for them. Or they
might be responsible for fund raising, which doesn't fit their personality. When everything is simple and easy for the leader, it can create a
type of boredom. When the leader is in an unfamiliar or uncomfortable area of leadership, it's anything but boring. It's more like terrifying.

Another reason for boredom may be because they have delegated
most of their tasks or responsibilities to other staff members. It's sort
of like the foreman who assigns responsibilities and tasks to their sub-
ordinates and then goes to their office, sits down at their desk, and

muses, "Well I've done my job in getting everyone to work. Now what am I going to do for the rest of the day?"

I would not suggest giving away all your tasks or responsibilities. If you do that, a type of emptiness and lack of involvement will arise. As a leader you need some tasks that are yours and yours alone. You need those for the sake of being able to contribute and to feel a sense of personal accomplishment. When you lose self-fulfillment in a job well done...boredom is lurking around the corner.

Boredom sometimes occurs when the leader gets wrapped up in and overwhelmed by administrative tasks, details, and stacks of paperwork. Usually you first begin a job as a laborer or in a very small leadership role. During this period you have lots of "frontline" or "hands on" ministry, service, or involvement. As you take on larger leadership

Everyone has some Hands On Work and Some Administration Work

Hands On Work
The Joy of being on the Front Line and actually being Involved

Administration
Responsibility
And Accountability
Increases as One Rises

WHEN YOU FIRST START

rolls, the "administrative details and functions" increase. You end up doing the paperwork and lose the fun, excitement, and experience of being where the action is. The more administrative functions increase and the further away you move from the action, the more opportunity for boredom to creep in.

Everyone gets bored with his or her job occasionally. When boredom is continual or long-term, it's probably a sign that the leader has grown personally larger than the job and (or) has lost the challenge of the job.

When the job is bigger and challenging for the employee, the more likely the employee will remain with the organization. When the employee is the same size as the job, some uneasiness develops. The employee begins to ask, *How long am I going to remain in this static job? Is there any future for me in this role? Can I see myself doing this job for the rest of my life?*

If the employee outgrows the job or does not feel challenged by the job, it is only a matter of time before they will leave the organization. They will begin to search elsewhere for challenge, mission, or personal development. Their boredom with the present position will drive them to seek fulfillment elsewhere.

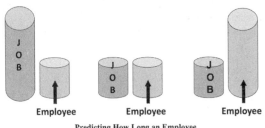

**Predicting How Long an Employee
Will Remain Working for an Organization**

Perhaps the world's second worst crime is boredom.
The first is being a bore.

~ JEAN BAUDRILLARD

Are you bored in your leadership role? It might be good for you to search out the cause. Destroying boredom begins with challenge and action. If you are not presently bored, then rejoice and be thankful. Boredom is indeed a great torture. If you don't believe me, ask your son or daughter who complains, "I'm bored."

> For the LORD gives [skillful and godly] wisdom; From His mouth come knowledge and understanding. He stores away sound wisdom for the righteous [those who are in right standing with Him]...

And He preserves the way of His saints (believers). Then you will understand righteousness and justice [in every circumstance] and integrity and every good path. For [skillful and godly] wisdom will enter your heart and knowledge will be pleasant to your soul. Discretion will watch over you, Understanding *and* discernment will guard you (Proverbs 2:6-11).

Dear Lord, ————————————————————————

I must admit that at times I've been bored at my job. Please help me evaluate what's prompting the boredom. If I'm the cause of my own boredom, please reveal that to me. Help me to take action. Help me to accept challenge and grow in areas where I'm weak. Help me to examine if the job is bigger than I am or if I'm bigger than my present job. Direct me if I need to consider moving toward a new and different vocation. Help me to be aware of the same struggle others may be going through. Help me not to be a boring leader.

————————————————————————— *Amen*

LEADERSHIP SUCCESS

Man is so unhappy that he would be bored even if he had no cause for boredom, by the very nature of his temperament, and he is so vain that though he has a thousand and one basic reasons for being bored, the slightest thing, like pushing a ball with a billiard cue, will be enough to divert him.

~BLAISE PASCAL

15

Sharpening Your Focus

People think focus means saying yes to the thing you've
got to focus on. But that's not what it means at all.
It means saying no to the hundred other good ideas
that there are. You have to pick carefully.

~Steve Jobs

Have you ever thought, *I wish I could live my life over again?* When Nadine Stair was 86 years old, she wrote these words:

> If I had my life to live over again, I'd dare to make more mis-takes next time. I'd relax. I'd limber up. I'd be sillier than I've been this trip. I would take fewer things seriously. I would take more chances, I would take more trips, I would climb more mountains and swim more rivers. I would eat more ice cream and less beans. I would, perhaps, have more actual troubles but fewer imaginary ones. You see, I'm one of those people who was sensible and sane, hour after hour, day after day.
>
> Oh, I've had my moments. If I had it to do over again, I'd have more of them. In fact, I'd try to have nothing else—just moments, one after another, instead of living so many years ahead of each day. I've been one of those persons who never goes anywhere with-out a thermometer, a hot-water bottle, a raincoat, and a para-chute. If I could do it again, I would travel lighter than I have.
>
> If I had my life to live over, I would start barefoot earlier in the spring and stay that way later in the fall. I would go to more dances, I would ride more merry-go-rounds, I would pick more daisies.

Guess what? There are no do overs. You only have one life to live. You can't start afresh. This is it. Now is the time to pick more daisies. Now is the time to make big goals. Now is the first day of the rest of your life.

The following chart is a general overview of the rest of your life. At the top of the chart, you will note "Your Present Age." At the bottom of the chart you will see the approximate number of "Productive Years Left." The questions are: How are you going to live those productive years? What are your plans for the future? What do you need to change in order to fulfill your plans?

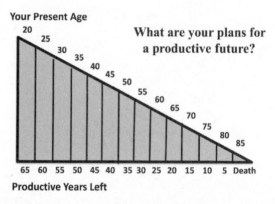

What would you like to experience? What would you like to learn or be part of in the days ahead? Is there something you would like to shape or change as a leader before you run out of time? Will there be something you leave behind that will be better than what you found?

Regardless of your age, you can do more than you think. You may desire to go back to school but think you're too old. You may see a need to retrain for a new vocation but think it would take too much time. You may want to move to a new area of the country but think you can't afford it. You may desire to change in several ways but think it will take too much energy. You may long to try something different but are afraid. Theodore Roosevelt said, "If we are to be really great people, we must strive in good faith to play a great part in the world. We cannot avoid meeting great issues. All that we can determine for ourselves is whether we shall meet them well or ill."

Let's imagine you would like to go back to school to get a degree. It will take time, and you'll probably have to go to night school. It may take two to four years of your life. Charles Buxton said, "You will never find time for anything. If you want time you must make it." It will take money for tuition and books. Returning to school takes a whole lot of energy—especially if you have to work during the day, go to school at night, and study on the weekends. Do you think you're too old?

Let me ask you a question. How old are you right now? All right, here is another question: If you don't go to school, how old will you be in four years? How old will you be in four years if you do go to school? Either way, you will be four years older. Do you want to be four years older with an education or four years older without an education? That's the real question. Time flies, but you are the navigator. Each moment you put off making decisions, life is passing you by.

> Great minds have purpose, others have wishes.
>
> ~ WASHINGTON IRVING

The next step for taking charge of your life is to focus on goals you would like to accomplish. Until you write down your goals and begin to act on them, they are only dreams.

Following are ten areas for which you may want to write some goals. Take time and list what you would like to see accomplished in each category. Make the goals as specific as possible. For example, instead of writing "I will read more," make it specific: "I will read 20 books this year."

You will need to revisit and renew your goals about every six months. This gives you the opportunity to cross off the goals you have reached and add new ones to the list. Keep a list of all the goals you accomplish. This will help you to realize the power of goal setting and encourage you to continue setting them.

You're in a position to lead other people and give them direction. How are you doing in leading and giving direction in your own life?

> Blessed [fortunate, prosperous, and favored by God] is the man who does not walk in the counsel of the wicked [following their advice and example], nor stand in the path of

sinners, nor sit [down to rest] in the seat of scoffers (ridicul-
ers). But his delight is in the law of the LORD, and on His
law [His precepts and teachings] he [habitually] meditates
day and night. And he will be like a tree *firmly* planted [and
fed] by streams of water, which yields its fruit in its season;
its leaf does not wither; and in whatever he does, he pros-
pers [and comes to maturity] (Psalm 1:1-3).

Spiritual Goals

1._____

2._____

3._____

4._____

5._____

Goals with Spouse

1._____

2._____

3._____

4._____

5._____

Goals with Children

1._____

2._____

3._____

4._____

5._____

Educational Goals

1._____
2._____
3._____
4._____
5._____

Vocational Goals

1._____
2._____
3._____
4._____
5._____

Financial Goals

1._____
2._____
3._____
4._____
5._____

Service Goals

1._____
2._____
3._____
4._____
5._____

Community Goals

1._____
2._____
3._____
4._____
5._____

Personal Goals

1._____
2._____
3._____
4._____
5._____

Miscellaneous Goals

1._____
2._____
3._____
4._____
5._____

Dear Lord,

It is so easy to get distracted in life and forget about the goals I would like to accomplish. The tyranny of the urgent and demanding things force out the important things I should be doing. Help me to focus on the future rather than mulling over the past and things I wish would have been different. Help me to accept things as they are and not dwell on how I wish they would be. Please help me to be grounded in the here and now of life and to learn to become a faithful and good leader. Help me to be obedient to You this day.

Amen

LEADERSHIP SUCCESS

Make no little plans; they have no magic to stir men's blood and probably themselves will not be realized. Make big plans; aim high in hope and work, remembering that a noble, logical diagram once recorded will never die, but long after we are gone will be a living thing, asserting itself with ever-growing insistency. Remember that your sons and grandsons are going to do things that would stagger us.

~ DANIEL H. BURNHAM

Stop getting distracted by things that have nothing to do with your goals.

~ R.E. PHILLIPS

You don't get results by focusing on results. You get results by focusing on the actions that produce results.

~ MIKE HAWKINS

Always remember your focus determines your reality.

~ GEORGE LUCAS

16

Moving Beyond Your Fears

*A day can really slip by when you're deliberately avoiding
what you're supposed to do.*

~ BILL WATTERSON

The day for Wayne Kroeker's retirement finally arrived. He had been the CEO of the Wilson Manufacturing Company for 12 years. Under his leadership the company experienced a series of ups and downs. Although Wayne was considered a nice guy, many of the upper level employees were not disappointed he was leaving.

They had struggled with Wayne and his decision-making ability. When it came to making a hard call, he consistently would put off making the decision. At his going away retirement party, his staff gave him a waffle iron with the impression of four different squares on the iron. He was a little bewildered with the gift at first and then laughed with everyone else. He got the subtle message.

Why do leaders sometimes struggle with decision-making? There are at least five major reasons. The first is *fear of the unknown*. The leader may not have knowledge or experience concerning the decision at hand. He or she may be looking for some sort of assurance or even a guarantee their decision will be the right one. You've probably heard someone say, "I don't want to make a decision until I get all of the facts." Of course, it's important to collect as much information as possible about any decision. However, if you wait until you get all the facts, it will no longer be a decision. It will be a conclusion. Decisions are made without all the facts. That's why they're called decisions.

The second reason for putting off a decision is *fear of failure*. No one wants to fail in front of his or her followers, friends, or family. No one wants to make the wrong choice. No one wakes up in the morning and says, "I hope I make lots of mistakes and poor decisions today." Public embarrassment is not something people aspire to. No leader deliberately wants to be wrong.

The third reason for hesitating is *fear of rejection*. Leaders are no different from those who are not in leadership positions. Everyone wants to be liked and appreciated. No one looks forward to being criticized, made a laughingstock, or separated from the group. Those in leadership positions instinctively know that not everyone will be pleased with their decision. They know decision-making is not part of a popularity contest. The leader is alone in their final decision. Their decision could affect the lives and finances of many people. Any sane person would naturally feel hesitation in making the final call.

The fourth factor in putting off a decision is because of a *fear of commitment*. When you commit to a task or a decision, you take responsibility for that task or decision. It's common and understandable that people shy away from accountability. It has been my experience that one of the striking places where you see the avoidance of responsibility and accountability is within governmental agencies. Often the person you're dealing with passes the final decision on to someone else for approval. Decisions move from one department to another, and time for decision-making drags on. The reason I want you to help me make a decision is that when everything goes wrong, I can turn back to you—you talked me into it!

The fifth reason is rather subtle. It's the *fear of success*. If the leader makes a good decision and everything turns out in a positive light, it sets a standard and expectation that must continually be exceeded. Who can live up to the high mark of always making the right decisions and never any poor or wrong decisions? The pressure becomes overwhelming and creates a desire to move away from being always responsible and accountable for future events.

Decision-making is not an easy task. Leaders are not promised a rose garden where everything is sunny and bright and every decision is right. As a leader you're hired to make decisions. If everyone else makes decisions for you, then you are not needed. Our families, our schools, our businesses, our community, and our government desperately need leaders who are responsible and accountable decision makers.

> This Book of the Law shall not depart from your mouth, but you shall read [and meditate on] it day and night, so that you may be careful to do [everything] in accordance with all that is written in it; for then you will make your way prosperous, and then you will be successful. Have I not commanded you? Be strong and courageous! Do not be terrified or dismayed (intimidated), for the LORD your God is with you wherever you go (Joshua 1:8-9).

Dear Lord,

I'm feeling the responsibility and accountability for my decisions within my circle of family, friends, and fellow workers. You know I want to make good decisions. Please help me to make the right decisions even in the possible face of failure and rejection by others. I know that Jesus had to make some unpopular decisions. He had the advantage, though, by being God in a human body. I know I'm not perfect as He is. Nevertheless, give me wisdom to make courageous decisions that will bring honor and glory to You.

Amen

LEADERSHIP SUCCESS

My father was my idol. I tried to emulate him not only as an ideal soldier but as a great man.

He used to say: "Gather all the facts possible and then make your decision on what you think is right, as opposed to what you think is wrong. Don't try to guess what others will think, whether they will praise or deride you. And always remember that at least some of your decisions will probably be wrong. Do this and you always will sleep well at night."

~ DOUGLAS MACARTHUR

17

Overcoming Worry

*Control your thoughts. Decide about that which you
will think and concentrate upon.
You are in charge of your life to the degree that
you take charge of your thoughts.*

~ EARL NIGHTINGALE

Heather had just received a promotion. She was now the new director of advertising at the Fargo Corporation. She had been the assistant to the director for three years and was both excited and anxious about her new position. She was a little uneasy as to how her fellow workers would respond to her now that she moved up the ladder of success. She had concerns about leading meetings, developing a budget, being creative, and fostering new ideas for advertising. She began to find herself worrying more than she used to.

Antonio Gaskin was one of the construction foremen for Wilson Homes. Both he and Duane Morse had held similar positions for about seven years. For quite some time both men had a difficult time getting along with each other. Duane had said a few things about Antonio that were damaging to his reputation. When Duane was chosen to become the construction superintendent for Wilson Homes, it was a difficult pill for Antonio to swallow. Instead of he and Duane being on the same level, Duane was now Antonio's boss.

Several months after Duane's promotion, Antonio began to realize that he was experiencing a mild form of depression. He found himself daydreaming and sighing a lot. Enthusiasm for his job began to taper off and going to work each day began to be increasingly uncomfortable.

Both Heather and Antonio were dealing with the very common emotions of anxiety and depression.

Heather ⟵————————————⟶ Antonio

ANXIETY   CONTROL   DEPRESSION

Anxiety is basically fear about future events: *Will I be able to do the job? Will I be accepted by my peers? What are the expectations?*

Depression is basically hurt and anger over past events: loss of promotion; negative comments about reputation; general uneasiness in the relationship.

A thread runs through and connects both anxiety and depression. That thread is the word *control.* The anxious person wants to control their future. The depressed person wishes they could control their past.

Guess what? There's no control going either way.

Being anxious does not change anything about the future. Being depressed does not change anything about the past. If you're anxious, how's that working out for you? If you are depressed, is your depression changing past hurts and angers? Do you feel like you're trapped in an emotional box with no way out?

Maybe it's time to change your plan of attack in dealing with these issues. Maybe it is time to turn away from the negative and look at the positive. The apostle Paul suggests:

> Don't worry about anything; instead, pray about everything; tell God your needs and don't forget to thank him for his answers. If you do this, you will experience God's peace, which is far more wonderful than the human mind can understand. His peace will keep your thoughts and your hearts quiet and at rest as you trust in Christ Jesus.

And now, brothers, as I close this letter let me say this one more thing: Fix your thoughts on what is true and good and right. Think about things that are pure and lovely, and dwell on the fine, good things in others. Think about all you can praise God for and be glad about. Keep putting into practice all you learned from me and saw me doing, and the God of peace will be with you (Philippians 4:6-9 TLB).

Dear Lord,

Please help me not to be an anxious leader or a depressed leader. Those who follow me and my family deserve much better. Help me to change my focus away from the past and the future and to focus on the present and how I can be a godly person today regardless of my circumstances. I confess that I often strive to control the various situations I find myself in. Please forgive me for attempting to take Your place as ruler of the universe. Not only is that impossible, but I haven't been very effective at it so far. Please help me to learn to trust in You and abide in You daily.

Amen

LEADERSHIP SUCCESS

If you want favor with both God and man, and a reputation for good judgment and common sense, then trust the Lord completely; don't ever trust yourself. In everything you do; put God first, and he will direct you and crown your efforts with success.

PROVERBS 3:5-6 TLB

18

The Loneliness of Leadership

*The whole conviction of my life now rests upon the belief
that loneliness, far from being a rare and curious phenomenon,
peculiar to myself and to a few other solitary men,
is the central and inevitable fact of human existence.*

~ THOMAS WOLFE

Have you ever felt lonely? Of course you have. Everyone alive has experienced the feeling of loneliness. It's been said that solitude is the joy of being alone and loneliness is the pain of being alone.

When it comes to leadership, loneliness is attached to the position. It's been said that loneliness is the other side of the coin of leadership. The mere fact that you're leading sets you apart—separates you—from others. That setting apart often has a certain sense of loneliness attached to it.

During my time as the executive director of a large youth camping operation, we had 130 year-round employees and up to 450 part-time employees. When I became the director, I could sense a change in conversations when I entered a room with other employees present. The leader had entered the room. Of course I wanted to be a normal person like everyone else. I wanted to be a part of the group, but my position changed all of that. You, as a leader, cannot be buddy-buddy with everyone that works under your leadership. An element of loneliness always comes with the job.

Jules Ormont suggests, "A ship, to run a straight course, can have but one pilot and one steering wheel. The same applies to the successful operation of a business. There cannot be a steering wheel at every seat in an organization."

Do you remember the story of Moses from the Old Testament? He was chosen to lead the nation of Israel out of bondage to the freedom of the Promised Land. Often he was forced to stand alone in his leadership decisions.

You would think that the nation (his followers) would be grateful he was leading them to escape the Egyptians who had enslaved them. Think again. They griped, complained, and criticized throughout the journey.

Other leaders rose up and attempted to overthrow Moses's leadership. Does that sound familiar? Moses's own brother and sister challenged him and made his job more difficult. Moses was called upon to be a judge and settle disputes between families and neighbors. Do you think those actions were appreciated by everyone involved? His followers threatened to revolt against his leadership. At one point even Moses's wife called him a "bridegroom of blood" (Exodus 4:25 NASB). Talk about feeling completely separated and alone.

Toward the end of his leadership career, Moses grew angry with all the criticism and complaints. He struck a rock when God had told him to speak to the rock. The end result? Moses was not able to complete his leadership role of leading the nation into the Promised Land. Yet, through all the turmoil, God called Moses His friend.

The worst part of being strong is that no one asks if you are okay.

General Colin Powell sums up the loneliness of command by saying, "Harry Truman was right. Whether you're a CEO or the temporary head of a project team, the buck stops here. You can encourage participative management and bottom-up employee involvement, but ultimately the essence of leadership is the willingness to make the tough, unambiguous choices that will have an impact on the fate of the organization. I've seen too many non-leaders flinch from this responsibility.

Even as you create an informal, open, collaborative corporate culture, prepare to be lonely."

Vision begins with one individual and is conveyed to others. Having a vision does not ensure that everyone will understand the vision or support it. Hold fast and continue to communicate with enthusiasm.

Having a mission and a burden does not mean that everyone will be aligned with that mission or burden. Hold fast and continue to communicate with concern.

Being committed and full of energy toward a goal does not mean that everyone has the same get-up-and-go. Hold fast and encourage participation.

One of the loneliest and most difficult parts of leadership is found in the constant griping, complaining, and criticism of you. Sometimes you have to keep your goal in mind and ignore all the barking. Winston Churchill said, "You will never reach your destination if you stop and throw stones at every dog that barks."

> The dogs bark, and the wagon rolls on.
> Wolves don't lose sleep over the opinion of sheep.

But whatever *former* things were gains to me [as I thought then], these things [once regarded as advancements in merit] I have come to consider as loss [absolutely worthless]

for the sake of Christ [and the purpose which He has given my life]...Not that I have already obtained it [this goal of being Christlike] or have already been made perfect, but I actively press on so that I may take hold of that [perfection] for which Christ Jesus took hold of me *and* made me His own. Brothers and sisters, I do not consider that I have made it my own yet; but one thing *I do*: forgetting what *lies* behind and reaching forward to what *lies* ahead, I press on toward the goal to win the [heavenly] prize of the upward call of God in Christ Jesus (Philippians 3:7,12-14).

Dear Lord,

Wow. The calling of leadership is not easy. In the past I have struggled with the loneliness of the position. I'm sure there's more loneliness to come. Give me the insight, courage, and strength to be a leader of integrity. Help me to stand by my morals and convictions even when the crowd does not agree. Please give me the patience and fortitude to put up with complaints and criticisms. Help me to learn to love those who disagree with me and make it difficult for me as a leader. Help me to realize that I'm not really alone. You are with me. You understand loneliness because all Your disciples left You. You understand complaints and criticisms. You faced them all the time. Help me to be kind and gentle, and to follow Your example.

Amen

LEADERSHIP SUCCESS

Leadership, at times, is lonely, because you must be out front, ahead of the followers. Also, because the leader is the one with the guiding vision and purpose, he/she sees the end from the beginning and must live both the process and the destination, all at the same time.

~ WILL MORELAND

A true leader has the confidence to stand alone, the courage to make tough decisions and the compassion to listen to the needs of others. He does not set out to be a leader but becomes one by the quality of his actions and the integrity of his intent. In the end, leaders are much like eagles; they don't flock—you find them one at a time.

~ DOUGLAS MACARTHUR

19

Mastering Your Emotions

Feelings are much like waves,
we can't stop them from coming
but we can choose which ones to surf.

–Jonatan Martensson

How do I change my emotions? If we must let go of hurt and anger, how do we do it?

Recently I was reminded of 2 Corinthians 2:1, which reads, "So I made up my mind that I would not make another painful visit to you" (NIV). As I began to ponder this verse, I realized that Paul was saying he could make up his mind (an act of the will) to change his emotions. How is it done? What is the process?

God created us with a mind, a will, and emotions. These three are separate, yet they interlock, overlap, and interplay with each other.

Mind: the thinking side of our being

Will: the volitional of doing side of our being

Emotions: the feeling side of our being

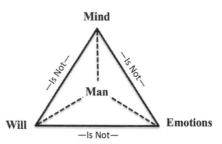

Many people live on an emotional level only. They are swayed, overpowered, and controlled by their emotions or feelings. The apostle Paul suggests that it's possible to live on a different level.

I will try to illustrate a very complicated and involved process. In the illustration that follows, you will note the dotted arrows leading from the emotions to the mind and the will. The dotted lines indicate that the emotions do not have direct control over the mind or the will. Your emotions have only indirect control; they send out feelings and suggestions to the will and to the mind. For example, you don't "feel good," so your emotions say, "Don't go to work." Or you don't "feel good," so your emotions say, "You must not be good. Your mind is wrong in thinking otherwise."

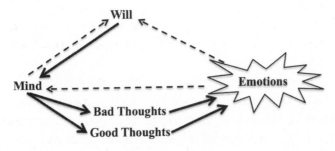

Similarly, you will note that the mind does not have direct control over the will, but indirect control. The solid arrows indicate that the will has direct control over the mind, and the mind has direct control over the emotions. If your mind thinks good or positive thoughts, you will have good emotions (feelings). If your mind thinks bad or negative thoughts, you will have bad emotions (feelings). We cannot think good thoughts and have bad emotions or think bad thoughts and have good emotions. Reality just doesn't work that way.

Imagine a large pink elephant with a blue ribbon around his neck. He is standing atop a car of a freight train as it rolls down the railroad track. Can you see his large ears flapping in the wind? Can you see him toss his trunk around and trumpet as the train moves along? It's a rather humorous but pleasant scene, isn't it? But now a problem arises. The train is heading for a tunnel. There is only enough room for the boxcars to make it through the opening. You can almost feel the impact (pardon the pun) of the situation.

Now, forget completely the scene of the elephant on the train. Erase it from your mind. Pause in your reading and try to do this. Do you still see him?

I now want you to imagine a small gray kitten playing on the floor in front of you as you read. He is playing with a ball of yellow yarn. See him swat the ball with his front paws? Look! There goes the ball rolling under the table.

What is the value of this exercise? I want you to realize the fact that when you see the gray kitten, you no longer see the pink elephant. Or vice versa. You can't see both pictures completely at the same time. This is true of your mind. If you think good thoughts, you have good corresponding emotions.

Let me proceed to make a more important point. *The will does not have direct control over the emotions; the will has direct control only over the mind.*

Can you think of someone who has hurt you—someone you are having a hard time forgiving? As you do this, you may feel some negative emotions rising, even if this hurt happened long ago. The more you think about this hurt, the higher your negative feelings rise.

> Feelings don't die easily because we keep
> feeding them with memories.
> That's exactly the reason it is so hard to move on.

Have you ever said to yourself, *I shouldn't feel this way? I'll change the way I feel toward this person?* It will never work! Your will does not have direct control over your emotions. Your will has direct control only over your mind. The only way you can change your emotions is by changing what your mind thinks about. It's exactly like the example of the pink elephant and the gray kitten.

> Anger is the emotion we snatch up
> to avoid less comfortable feelings
> like confusion, hurt, fear, and sadness.
>
> ~Alan Wolfelt

What do you think makes heroes in battle? It's not the mind. The mind says, "If I go out there to rescue my friend, the odds are I'll be shot." It's not the emotions. The emotions say, "If I go out there and get shot, it will hurt, and I don't like to hurt." It's the will that motivates the hero. The will overrides both the mind and the emotions.

Have you ever felt like *not* praising the Lord? Have you ever felt like *not* forgiving someone? Have you been overpowered by your angry emotions? You can change all of that if you want to. You have within your being the power to change how you feel. It comes by an exercise of your will. Change what your mind is thinking about and you will change your emotions. I didn't say it was easy, but it is possible. If you want success as a leader, learn to master your emotions.

> And now brothers, as I close this letter let me say this one more thing. Fix *[an act of the will]* your thoughts *[the mind]* on what is true and good and right. Think *[the mind]* about things that are pure and lovely, and dwell on the fine, good things in others. Think *[the mind]* about all you can praise God for and be glad about. Keep putting into practice *[an act of the will]* all you learned from me and saw me doing, and the God of peace *[an emotional experience]* will be with you (Philippians 4:8-9 TLB, emphases mine).

Dear Lord, ——————————————————

I fully realize that I have a host of conflicting emotions and thoughts. Sometimes my emotions seem out of control like a wild runaway horse. I desperately need Your help in learning how to bridle my feelings. I also find that my mind switches from one topic to another, and it's hard to slow down that process. Teach me to exercise my will and grant the courage to put forth effort to change what I'm thinking about. Help me to learn the habit of mastering my emotions. Help me to corral good thoughts and shoo away negative thinking.

———————————————————   *Amen*

LEADERSHIP SUCCESS

You cannot make yourself feel something you do not feel,
but you can make yourself do right in spite of your feelings.

~PEARL S. BUCK

20

How Will You Respond?

There's a strong victim mentality in my generation.
I think it's spiritual laziness.
They will agree that God is sovereign over all,
but then they will say, "Well, I wish he would
sovereignly take away my lust issue." There's just not
a lot of fortitude, not a lot of fight in them.

~ Matt Chandler

In general, there are two types of people in this world: those who are controlled by life's events and circumstances, and those who attempt to control their lives and their destinies.

The first could be likened to thermometers that *register* the temperature [atmosphere and events] around them. The others are like thermostats, which *regulate* the temperature [atmosphere and events] of their lives.

The first group sees itself as a *victim* of circumstances, and the other sees itself as a *player* in the circumstances. Victims make excuses; players make changes. Victims think the events that occur in their lives are the important issue. Players believe that how they think about and respond to the events is more important than the events themselves. Victims think circumstances determine life and mental health. Players believe attitude determines life and mental health.

It's easy to identify victims because their lives are in a continual state of drama. They feel they have a *right* to complain and tell everyone they can about their problems. Although they are often quiet and brooding, they know their behavior will attract the attention they seek. When they don't get the attention, they wallow in self-pity.

Victims are not very resilient. They have very little staying power or endurance. They give up easily when things don't go their way. They have an undercurrent of anger in their lives caused by what they think is undeserved heartache. They avoid owning any responsibility for their circumstances and shun accountability for their actions. With all the drama surrounding them, people tend to avoid them. People have heard the victim story many times before—and enough is enough.

Dr. Laura Schlessinger aptly identifies the situation when she says, "When you're the victim of the behavior, it's black and white; when you're the perpetrator, there are a million shades of gray."

One day a woman stopped me and asked for my advice about a matter. She had only 15 minutes to talk. She began to tell me about her divorce. It had occurred two years before, and she was having a hard time adjusting to all the hurt. As I listened I glanced at my watch and realized she had been talking for about 8 minutes of the 15.

I began to think, "How can I help her in seven minutes?"

I interrupted her unloading of hurt and said, "So what."

It shocked her, and she asked, "What do you mean, so what?"

I replied, "How many people have you talked with today about your divorce?"

She hesitated. "Including you?"

"Yes, including me."

"Several, I guess."

I said, "If I talked to several people a day for two years about my divorce, I would have difficulty getting over it too. You need to let go of all of your hurt, stop talking to other people about your divorce, and get on with life." (I haven't had a divorce.) She had developed a pattern of constantly thinking and talking about being the victim of a divorce. It was time for her to take control of her emotions and accept the reality that her marriage was over and there was nothing she could do about it.

How do you see yourself at this time in your life? Are you the victim or are you the strong player? As a leader it's your job to lead. You are the thermostat. You are the regulator of the circumstances in most cases. Victims do not make good leaders because their driving force is to have everyone meet their needs and desires.

Listed below is a practical checklist for Victims and Players. Look it over and see how you match up.

VICTIMS	PLAYERS
Wishful thinking	Practical thinking
Immediate gratification	Delayed gratification
Ease	Work
Withdrawal	Involvement
Lack of goals	Goal setting
Powerless	Powerful
Give up easily	Persistent
Low self-esteem	Healthy self-esteem
Give in to temptation	Resist temptation
Discouraged	Enthusiastic
Undisciplined	Disciplined
Wait for opportunity	Create opportunity

For this very reason, applying your diligence [to the divine promises, make every effort] in [exercising] your faith to, develop moral excellence, and in moral excellence, knowledge (insight, understanding), and in *your* knowledge, self-control, and in *your* self-control, steadfastness, and in *your* steadfastness, godliness, and in *your* godliness, brotherly affection, and in *your* brotherly affection, [develop Christian] love [that is, learn to unselfishly seek the best for others and to do things for their benefit] (2 Peter 1:5-7).

Dear Lord, ──────────────────────

It's easy to fall into victim mentality when I undergo gossip, criticism, and unfairness. My natural reaction is to want to get revenge upon those who have hurt me. Help me to realize that You are not caught off guard by any of the circumstances in my life. Help me to change my attitude about problems and difficulties. Please give me the wisdom and strength to choose to become a player in the situations of life rather than a victim.

Help me to become a positive thermostat leader rather than a thermometer that only measures hurt and pain. Please use me to assist others who may be struggling in this area. I want to be sensitive to Your leading and be used by You.

Amen

LEADERSHIP SUCCESS

You only have control over three things in your life—the thoughts you think, the images you visualize, and the actions you take.

~ JACK CANFIELD

21

The Ugly Side of Leadership

The price one pays for pursuing any profession or calling is an intimate knowledge of its ugly side.

~ JAMES BALDWIN

Well, I didn't promise you a rose garden, did I? Very few books touch on the messiness encountered in leadership. When we talk about the ugly side, many people might think we're talking about something wicked, evil, or unprincipled. Occasionally as a leader you may encounter something immoral, unlawful, or illegal. That's a difficult matter for sure, and it requires courage and determination to stand against corruption. But that type of ugliness is straightforward and easy to identify. The ugliness I'm referring to is not quite as clear and open.

There is a subtle ugliness that is very unbecoming, nasty, and even dangerous. This ugliness occurs as people interact with each other. It takes the form of complaints, criticisms, and disagreements as to methods, philosophy, and those in authority. It can lead to finger pointing, gossip, and destroying the reputations of others. It can create factions, division, and the choosing of sides.

Office politics, political correctness, and the pressure or threat to conform are not usually written in an employee handbook. Nevertheless, these are just as real.

Ugliness can take the form of confusion, disorganization, and a chaotic atmosphere. It can be found in doublespeak, weasel words, and misleading white lies. It sometimes takes the form of back-scratching, payoff, and sycophancy. The word *sycophancy* is not commonly used today. It involves flattery or fawning over someone. Some call it "sucking up" to those in authority. A sycophant is a "yes man" or "yes woman."

As I have traveled to other countries, I have asked those in our leadership seminars if they have a term for the word *sycophancy*. Listed below are a few of the responses.

- In Kenya they're called a *boot licker.*
- In Bolivia they're called a *sock sucker.*
- In Guatemala they're called a *flat chest* or a *snake.*
- In Papua New Guinea they're called a *grease man.*
- In Liberia they're called someone who gives *eye service.*
- In Nigeria they're called a *praise singer* or a *coattail puller.*
- In the United States there are many other names that are not proper to mention.

Authors and leadership experts Warren Bennis and Burt Nanus touch on this subject when they say, "What we have found is that the higher the rank, the more interpersonal and human the undertaking. Our top executives spend roughly 90 percent of their time concerned with the messiness of people problems."

James, the half brother of Jesus, touches on ugliness when he says:

> Men have trained, or can train, every kind of animal or bird that lives and every kind of reptile and fish, but no human being can tame the tongue. It is always ready to pour out its deadly poison. Sometimes it praises our heavenly Father, and sometimes it breaks out into curses against men who are made like God. And so blessing and cursing come pouring out of the same mouth. Dear brothers, surely this is not right! Does a spring of water bubble out first with fresh water and then with bitter water? Can you pick olives from a fig tree, or figs from a grape vine? No, and you can't draw fresh water from a salty pool.
>
> If you are wise, live a life of steady goodness so that only

good deeds will pour forth. And if you don't brag about them, then you will be truly wise! And by all means don't brag about being wise and good if you are bitter and jealous and selfish; that is the worst sort of lie. For jealousy and selfishness are not God's kind of wisdom. Such things are earthly, unspiritual, inspired by the devil. For wherever there is jealousy or selfish ambition, there will be disorder and every other kind of evil (James 3:7-16 TLB).

At some point in your leadership career, you will come face-to-face with the ugly side of your calling or profession. Don't be shocked. It's just a matter of time. The question is, "How are you going to deal with it? What should you do with the seeds of discontent, disorder, and disagreement?" The brother of Jesus suggests replacing ugly seeds with different seeds.

But the wisdom that comes from heaven is first of all pure and full of quiet gentleness. Then it is peace-loving and courteous. It allows discussion and is willing to yield to others; it is full of mercy and good deeds. It is wholehearted and straightforward and sincere. And those who are peacemakers will plant seeds of peace and reap a harvest of goodness (James 3:17-18 TLB).

Dear Lord,

Help me be on guard and prepared when I encounter the ugly side of my leadership calling. Give me the courage and determination to deal with offensive comments and behaviors. Help me to be a leader that roots out dissention and disruptive talk. Help me to eliminate jealousy and selfish ambition as much as is in my ability to do so. I want to be straightforward and sincere in my communication and leadership. Give me a gentle but firm spirit as I attempt to sow seeds of peace with those who follow me.

Amen

LEADERSHIP SUCCESS

The currency with which you pay for peace is made up of manly courage, fearless virility, readiness to serve justice and honor at any cost, and a mind and a heart attuned to sacrifice.

~ WILLIAM FRANKLIN KNOX

22

Getting the Monkey off Your Back

The best job goes to the person who can get it done
without passing the buck or coming back with excuses.

~ Napoleon Hill

Karen knocked on her supervisor's door. "Mr. Ortman, do you have a moment? I need your opinion and advice about a matter."

"Sure, Karen. Come on in. How can I help you?"

"Well, I've contacted the Shipping Department about a problem, and they seem to ignore my concerns. Some of our customers are not receiving their orders, and I don't know how to get those working in Shipping to address the situation. I thought you needed to know about it."

"Thanks, Karen. I'll check into it."

The question is, "Should Mr. Ortman check into it or not?" He is the supervisor, after all. Or has Mr. Ortman just been given a bait and switch technique by Karen? The bait was, "I need your opinion and advise about a matter." The switch occurred when Mr. Ortman said, "I'll check into it."

Karen switched the monkey (*problem*) that was on her back to Mr. Ortman's. He then accepted the monkey and said he would deal with it. The monkey was now on Mr. Ortman's back. Pretty cool deal, right?

As a leader it's not the best idea for you to readily become a zoo-keeper for everyone's monkey. Imagine what would happen if you had 25 people working for you and each one came with a problem for you to solve for them. What if you had 50 or more people working for you? Pretty soon your zoo would be overcrowded with monkeys.

Remember Moses in the Old Testament. All of the children of Israel came to him to be a judge for all of their problems and difficulties. When Moses's father-in-law saw this, he told Moses that the burden was too great for one man to bear alone. He told Moses that he would soon burn out with the pressure of so many decisions. Moses then began to delegate decision-making to more people.

Why do leaders get sucked into accepting other people's monkey problems? It might be for several reasons.

- Leaders want to be liked.
- Leaders want to be needed.
- Leaders may have a hard time saying no.
- Leaders may think they're the only one who is smart enough to handle the issue.
- Leaders may not trust the decision-making ability of their employees.
- Leaders might think the employee could make a mistake and mess up everything.
- Leaders might be the controlling type of person.
- Leaders might be afraid to give power to others.
- Leaders might think, "If I gave away decision-making to others, then what would I be doing?"

Have you ever been sucked in or tricked to accept the monkey that was on someone else's back? You might even have accepted it unknowingly. Now who is the boss? Who is doing all the work dealing with the monkey? Surely it's not Karen. She has not learned how to make decisions and how to work with others.

Many years ago I had a manager named John working for me. One day John came to me with a problem that needed to be solved. He asked, "How do you want this resolved?" I smiled and said, "John, I could make that decision, but I'm not going to. That's your decision. I trust you to make it. If I make all your decisions for you as a manager, then you're not really needed. I need you to make that decision."

John made a great decision and rose to become a very effective leader who learned to delegate decision-making to others.

Are you aware of some monkeys that need to be passed back to their original owner? Have you carried them long enough? Or do you have room on your back to carry more of them? Maybe it is time for you to help others to become decision makers and future leaders. Remember, part of your job as a leader is to help others become leaders also.

> The next day Moses sat as usual to hear the people's complaints against each other, from morning to evening. When Moses' father-in-law saw how much time this was taking, he said, "Why are you trying to do all this alone?...It's not right...You're going to wear yourself out—and if you do, what will happen to the people?...Find some capable, godly, honest men...and appoint them as judges (Exodus 18:13-21 TLB).

Dear Lord, ———————————————————————

Help me to realize that I cannot oversee every detail. Help me to surround myself with capable, godly, and honest men and women. Help me to be the type of leader unafraid to pass on decision-making to other leaders. Help me to be alert to their need to grow and become more effective leaders. Help me to learn how to gracefully turn down other people's monkeys that they should be carrying themselves. Also help me to pass back some of the monkeys I have taken on because of the wrong reasons.

Thank You in advance for helping me clean the zoo of unnecessary monkeys.

——————————————————————— *Amen*

LEADERSHIP SUCCESS

The best executive is the one who has sense enough to pick good men to do what he wants done, and the self-restraint enough to keep from meddling with them while they do it.

~ THEODORE ROOSEVELT

23

Getting Motivated

I am not a product of my circumstances.
I am a product of my decisions.

~ STEPHEN COVEY

Have you ever felt like not doing anything? Have you had a difficult time getting started on a task? Have you pondered what it would take to get motivated? Have you wondered where motivation comes from?

Understanding motivation is not brain surgery or astrophysics. It's not a complex science. In fact, it's very basic. The short answer is: *We do in life what we want to do.*

You might say, "Now wait a minute. There are a number of things I want to do but don't do them."

"Oh yeah. Like what?"

"Well, like why do I neglect mundane matters such as failing to clean out the garage, washing the windows, or writing letters to my relatives? Why do I tell lies when I know the truth? Why do I fail to seek to know God as I should?"

"You neglect to do things because you don't want to do them. You tell lies because you want to. And you don't seek God because you don't have an interest in doing so."

Life's Three Steps

Part of solving any problem is to understand just what the problem is. What motivates you to do anything in this life? The following chart may help you to understand human motivation.

OBJECTIVE	=	**Goal** or purpose to be achieved
MEANS	=	**Methods** used to reach the desired objective
EFFORT	=	**Energy** required, using means to reach the end

Example A

OBJECTIVE	Reduce and lose unnecessary weight
MEANS	1. Cut off your head and lose ten ugly pounds
	2. Stop eating
	3. Drink SlimFast
	4. Adopt the keto diet
	5. Sign up for Weight Watchers
	6. Go to Jenny Craig
	7. Eat smaller portions
	8. Die
EFFORT	An extreme amount

Example B

OBJECTIVE	To be first-string on the football team
MEANS	1. Block
	2. Tackle
	3. Hurt
	4. Study plays
	5. Bleed
EFFORT	A great deal of it

Example C

OBJECTIVE	To be a doctor
MEANS	1. Go to school forever
	2. Be a good listener

	3. Learn to write illegibly
	4. Learn to carve
	5. Learn how to make out bills clearly
EFFORT	An exceeding amount

Everything in life revolves around the principle of *Objective, Means, and Effort*. We cannot reach any objective—secular or spiritual—without using all three steps.

Do you believe that someone can lose weight without using means and effort? What do you think the football coach would say to a young man who wants to be a starter but doesn't attend practice? Or what about the woman who walks into the hospital and wants to perform an operation but has no training and experience? Do you think the medical staff would let her operate? This same principle applies to the Christian life: *Objective, Means,* and *Effort*.

OBJECTIVE	To be a Spirit-filled, Spirit-led, joyful Christian
MEANS	1. Receive Christ as Savior and Lord
	2. Study the Bible
	3. Pray
	4. Share your faith
	5. Seek fellowship with other believers
	6. Be obedient to the Holy Spirit
	7. Control anger, forgive others, and so forth
EFFORT	A vast amount

The Ultimate Question

As we look at the principle of *Objective, Means, and Effort*, other questions arise. What determines the amount of effort expended, using the means, to reach the objective? How do I get motivated?

The worth of the objective determines the amount of effort we put forth, using the means to reach the end. How much is it worth to you to reduce your weight; to be a starter; to be a cheerleader; to be a doctor; or to be a Spirit-filled, Spirit-led, joyful Christian? How much is it worth to learn how to deal with your anger? How much is it worth to gain peace by forgiving those who have sinned against you? If the objective is worthwhile to you, you *will* put forth the effort and use the available means in order to reach your goal. If it's not worth it to you...you won't do it.

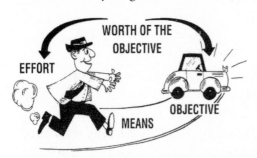

God's objective was our restored fellowship with Him. He put forth the effort, using the means (going to the cross in our place) to reach His end goal. It was worth it all. Jesus said:

> No one takes it from me, but I lay it down of my own accord (John 10:18 NIV).

Dear Lord,

Sometimes I get stuck thinking I really want to do something, but I don't put forth any effort to reach my goal. Help me to realize the plain truth that I don't move forward because it really isn't worth the effort, using the means to accomplish the task. Help me to face this truth honestly. Please help me, Lord, as I put forth the effort to keep my eyes on You and look to You for help and encouragement. I want to be more motivated. I want to hold high the worth of it all.

Amen

LEADERSHIP SUCCESS

Motivation is what gets you started. Habit is what keeps you going.

~ JIM RYUN

24

Facing the Facts

Most of the problems in life are because of two problems:
1. We act without thinking.
2. We keep thinking without acting.

Years ago I was involved in a head-on collision. I was driving a van on a two-lane highway, cruising about 55 miles per hour. As I approached an intersection, I could see a pickup approaching the same intersection from the right. I knew the truck would come to a stop sign before entering the highway.

In a split-second I realized that he had run the stop sign. Although I will take several paragraphs to explain what happened next, please remember the event occurred in milliseconds.

As the other driver entered the intersection, I thought he would keep going and I could miss him by veering to the right. But then the unbelievable happened. He stopped in the middle of the intersection, squarely in front of me, making it impossible to veer to the right and miss hitting him. My guess is that he didn't see me coming, but he saw a car in the left lane driving my direction and stopped for it to pass.

I knew that if I hit him by driving straight, I would most likely crush and kill him. The only place to turn was to the left, attempting to cross the other lane and enter a parking lot on that side of the highway. I thought I would miss the pickup and the oncoming car in the left lane, saving both lives even though I might crash into a building at the back of the parking lot.

However, it didn't work out that way. The driver in the oncoming car thought I was attempting to pass. He turned his car to let me pass, not realizing his move put both of us on the path of a head-on collision.

To make a long story short, the driver in the truck escaped all damage. The driver in the other car suffered minor injuries. I almost severed my arm. That event occurred over 20 years ago, but as a result I experience continual pain in my right arm.

What's the point of the story, you ask? The point is that the continual pain I feel is not a problem. It's a fact of life. Problems are things we can work on and change. Facts of life are something we must accept and make peace with, because we cannot change them.

My daughter is a Type 1 brittle diabetic. She has been diabetic since she was almost four years of age. That's not a problem. That's a fact of life. It's not something we can change. We must accept and make peace with it.

Another illustration: Two years ago I cut off my left thumb with a crosscut saw. Naturally, it was not the most pleasant of experiences. And it's now very difficult for me to fasten small buttons on my shirts. This is not a problem. It's not something I can change. It's something I must accept and make peace with. I need to adjust and move on with life.

How about you? Do you have some facts of life you have to make peace with and accept? As a leader you will encounter some difficulties that go far beyond problems you can work with and change.

You may recall the Serenity Prayer written by Reinhold Niebuhr.

> God grant me the serenity
> to accept the things I cannot change;
> courage to change the things I can;
> and wisdom to know the difference.

The above lines are quite famous and have been often quoted. What many people do not realize is that the prayer contains more than just the four lines. It continues as follows:

> Living one day at a time;
> enjoying one moment at a time;
> accepting hardships as the pathway to peace;

taking, as He did, this sinful world
as it is, not as I would have it;
trusting that He will make all things right
if I surrender to His Will;
that I may be reasonably happy in this life
and supremely happy with Him
forever in the next.
Amen.

Years before Reinhold Niebuhr wrote the Serenity Prayer, Mother Goose said,

For every ailment under the sun
There is a remedy or there is none,
If there be one try and find it,
If there be none, never mind it.

One day there was a contest between artists. They were asked to paint what they believed was a picture of peace and an escape from problems. Many of the artists drew pictures of landscapes with big white fluffy clouds, quiet streams of water, or pictures of sunrises and sunsets.

The winning artist drew a picture of a raging waterfall. In the midst of the waterfall was an outcropping of rock with a bird sitting on it, singing. The bird was not concerned with the problem of raging water all around. It was resting on the fact of the solid foundation of the rock. It was at peace.

Who shall ever separate us from the love of Christ? Will tribulation, or distress, or persecution, or famine, or nakedness, or danger or sword?…For I am convinced [and continue to be convinced—beyond any doubt] that neither death, nor life, nor angels, nor principalities, nor things present *and* threatening, nor things to come, nor powers, nor height, nor depth, nor any other created thing, will be able to separate us from the [unlimited] love of God, which is in Christ Jesus our Lord (Romans 8:35,38-39).

Dear Lord,

Help me to understand the difference between problems I can work on with Your help and facts of life I need to accept and make peace with. Sometimes I get wrapped up thinking about problems and doing nothing to resolve them. And on the other hand, Lord, I find myself fighting against facts of life that I need to accept. This next week please help me to be alert to facts of life that will not change. Help me to help others do the same thing. I look forward to some of the peace You want to give when I cease to fight against your will.

Amen

LEADERSHIP SUCCESS

I have learned that success is to be measured not so much by the position that one has reached in life as by the obstacles which he has overcome while trying to succeed.

~ BOOKER T. WASHINGTON

25

Breaking Out of Your Rut

It has been said that life is like a merry-go-round.
It just keeps turning in circles.

Have you ever felt like you're running around in circles like a dog chasing its tail but never quite able to catch it? Have you been under a lot of pressure with no relief in sight? Have you been injured by others and felt like escaping from all the hurt? Do you feel like a horse carrying a heavy burden?

Do you know how they deal with a horse that's wild and unbroken, or has been damaged because of some type of accident or trauma? You put it into the round pen.

A round pen is just like it sounds: It's a circled corral that is often covered with boards from the ground to about eight feet high. Imagine a round plywood wall that the horse cannot see over even if it rears up on its hind legs.

When the horse enters the round pen and the opening is shut, it begins to run around the walls of the pen. It's desperately seeking escape. The same thing happens the first time you bring home a new dog and put it into your backyard. It runs around the perimeter for several minutes before it begins to settle down.

As you watch the horse running around and around, you will notice several things. Its eyes are wide open and seem to have a terrified, wild look to them. The horse's ears are raised high and attentive. It is breathing hard, and snot is coming from its nostrils. Often, the horse is passing gas as it moves around the pen. One can easily tell it is not happy about being in the pen.

In the center of the pen is something that many horses are not aware of when they first enter. They're too busy trying to find a way out. Not until they begin to slow down, stop, and look about do they become aware they're not alone.

In the center of the pen is the trainer, who has been watching the horse run in circles. He or she has been patiently waiting for the horse to get tired. The trainer is waiting for the horse to stop and notice that someone has been there all the time, watching it.

When the horse becomes aware of the trainer, its ears perk up and it stares intently at the human. The trainer also looks into the eyes of the horse. For a moment or two, there's no movement. Then the trainer steps toward the horse.

The horse's head will quickly rise, its eyes will be wide, and its ears will go backward on its head. The horse will then turn and begin to run around the pen. The trainer will watch the horse and turn around following it until it calms down and again stares at the trainer. After a moment the trainer will take a step toward the horse. The horse will snort and begin running around the pen.

This same process can continue for 15 to 90 minutes. The trainer is waiting for the horse to finally get tired of running and passing gas. The trainer can tell when the horse has finally given up. It happens when he steps toward the horse and the horse doesn't move. He will then take a few more slow steps toward the horse. When he sees the horse's eyes begin to flash or the ears move back, he will stop and give the horse time to relax and get used to his presence in front of it.

When the trainer gets to about six feet in front of the horse, he will stop and make complete eye contact with the animal. His next move seems strange to anyone who might be watching the process. The trainer slowly turns around until his back is to the horse. Then he begins to walk away.

What do you think happens next? You guessed it. The horse begins to follow. Trust has been established and the training process has now begun.

In so many ways, we're like the horse. We often find ourselves running around and around in the pen of life, seeming to go nowhere and with no escape. Sometimes the pressures and demands of leadership seem overwhelming to us, and we would like to escape. Only when we stop running and take a moment to look around do we become aware we're not alone. Our Trainer has been there all the time. He's been waiting for us to get tired of all our fruitless efforts to break free.

The Trainer has been waiting for you to focus on Him and stop striving. He wants to draw close to you. He wants to lead you. He wants you to trust Him. Are you ready to follow, or do you need to run a little longer? It's okay. He'll wait for you. He's longing to catch your eye.

> Therefore then, since we are surrounded by so great a cloud of witnesses [who have borne testimony to the Truth], let us strip off *and* throw aside every encumbrance (unnecessary weight) and that sin which so readily (deftly and cleverly) clings to *and* entangles us, and let us run with patient endurance *and* steady *and* active persistence the appointed course of the race that is set before us,
>
> Looking away [from all that will distract] to Jesus, Who is the Leader *and* the Source of our faith [giving the first incentive for our belief] and is also its Finisher [bringing it to maturity and perfection]. He, for the joy [of obtaining the prize] that was set before Him, endured the cross, despising *and* ignoring the shame, and is now seated at the right hand of the throne of God.
>
> Just think of Him Who endured from sinners such grievous opposition *and* bitter hostility against Himself [reckon up and consider it all in comparison with your trials], so that you may not grow weary *or* exhausted, losing heart *and* relaxing *and* fainting in your minds (Hebrews 12:1-3 AMPC).

Dear Lord, ———————————————————————

I'm tired of running circles in the round pen. I'm tired of trying to escape from all my pressures, concerns, and hurts. I've tried to do it my way, but it doesn't seem to be working. Help me to be aware of Your presence. Help me to begin to focus on You instead of on my problems and difficulties. I want to become a leader who keeps his eyes on Jesus. I want to follow where You are leading. Thank You for loving and caring for me even when I run around in circles. I want the running to stop.

Amen

LEADERSHIP SUCCESS

When everything seems to be going against you, remember that the airplane takes off against the wind, not with it.

~ HENRY FORD

Dealing with Relational Conflicts

If you avoid conflict to keep the peace,
you start a war within yourself.

~CHERYL RICHARDSON

When someone goes fishing with a rod, it is called angling. The person is attempting to catch a fish. When someone goes fishing with an idea, it's also an attempt to catch something...an individual...and reel them in toward the fisherman's point of view. The one doing the fishing has a slant, a perspective, or a position. They would like another person to take the bait (emotional outlook) and be drawn to viewing events and situations in the same light as the fisherman does. This happens all the time. It's called "triangling." The news media has made triangling an art form.

Triangling often takes place when one person has a disagreement with another person or has been hurt by that person. We will call the person doing the triangling party A. We will call the person who disagrees with or has hurt Party A by the name of Party B. Triangling theory suggests that the person feeling the most discomfort in the relationship will invariably triangle a third party, called Party C.

Party A (Clara) has a problem with Party B (Rachel)
and involves Party C (Marsha)

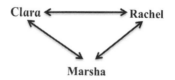

Clara is the one with the most discomfort or hurt. Rachel may or may not be aware of Clara's discomfort. Because of Clara's misgivings about Rachel, she will attempt to get Marsha on her side and to feel the same way about Rachel. Party C (Marsha) has some form of relationship with both Party A (Clara) and Party B (Rachel).

How does this happen? Clara will approach Marsha and say something such as: "Marsha, do you have a moment to talk?"

"I do have some time. How can I help you?" Marsha responds.

"You know Rachel, don't you?"

"I do. We've been friends for about a year and a half now."

"Well, I've got an issue with Rachael, and I don't know how to resolve it. I could use your wise advice and counsel." (Clara is beginning to set the hook into Marsha.)

At this point Clara will begin to slowly dump all her frustrations, anger, resentment, or bitterness about Rachel onto Marsha. "Did you know that she _____." "Are you aware that she _____." "I can't believe that she _____." And on and on Clara will speak as she dumps all her gossip and garbage about Rachel. She is attempting to draw Marsha to her point of view and to make Rachel look bad in the eyes of Marsha. In this way Clara and Marsha begin to form a united front against Rachel, which makes Rachael somewhat of an outcast.

Have you ever been triangled? My guess is that you will probably get triangled in some form within the next 30 days. Maybe in your home, at work, or with some form of community involvement, or even at your church.

To keep from being triangled, it's important to be able to balance the seriousness of the situation with the humor of the situation. In the case of Clara and Rachel, it's serious that two women are at odds with each other. It's also somewhat humorous that two adult women are unable to resolve a seemingly minor misunderstanding or hurt that may be resolved if they would simply talk with each other.

Seriousness   **Humor**

Balance

Marsha (Party C) could suggest: "I know Rachel and I know you. I think you could work the situation out if you would talk with her."

Clara would most likely have one or two responses. First, she might say, "No, that will not work! I've tried that before and it hasn't been successful."

The second response might be: "Thank you for your help and advice. I'll talk with her." Which is not true. Clara has no intention to talk with Rachel. She simply sees that Marsha is not jumping to her side of the story. She is now going to talk with someone more sympathetic to her case. Clara will attempt to "triangle" other people in order to spread more rumors, gossip, or hurtful comments about Rachel. The division begins to grow and spread. In a religious setting, such discord could be the beginning of a church split.

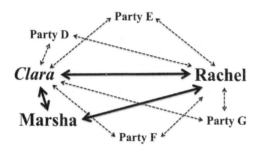

If you were to find yourself in Marsha's place, how would you deal with the situation between Clara and Rachel? Would you simply ignore it and hope that it would go away? It won't. It will only grow and may infect other employees as they began to choose sides.

You, as a leader, might say, "I can see that you're concerned about your relationship with Rachel and would like it resolved. And I bet Rachel would also like to see any negative issues cleared up." This helps to keep you neutral and balanced. "Since you came to me for help, let's both go over to Rachel's office and see if we can clear up any misunderstanding and resolve any issues that are hurting your relationship with each other."

My guess is that Clara will be a little shocked by that response. She may even say, "Now is not a good time" or "That won't be necessary." Why would she reply this way? Probably because she is afraid of the consequence of facing Rachel, or she really doesn't want to resolve the issue. What she wants to do is be mad at Rachel, get even with her, and hurt her reputation in some way.

Whether it's a woman or a man involved in triangling, don't pass by the opportunity to be a mediator, reconciler, and leader in the situation. The best time to settle disputes is as soon as possible. Don't let them grow.

> Any story sounds true until someone tells the other side and sets the record straight (Proverbs 18:17 TLB).

Dear Lord,

When people come to me with issues about other people, please help me to be discerning and realize there are two sides to every story. Give me the wisdom to know the difference between someone wanting true advice and direction and someone who just wants to vent bad feeling about someone else. Give me the ability to stay balanced and neutral so that I can be effective in helping people to resolve conflicts. Lord, help me not to become involved in "triangling." Help me to quickly resolve issues and problems I might have with someone. Help me to become a peacemaker.

Amen

LEADERSHIP SUCCESS

The most essential quality for leadership is not perfection but credibility. People must be able to trust you.

~ RICK WARREN

27

Changing Your World

No person was ever honored for what he received.
Honor has been the reward for what he gave.

~ Calvin Coolidge

D r. Karl Menninger, the famous psychiatrist who founded the Menninger Clinic, was one day asked how to prevent a nervous breakdown. He suggested that the best way would be to pull down all the shades in your house, turn off all the lights, lock all of the doors, and "go across the railroad tracks and find someone in need and do something for him."

It is easy to become so focused on our own problems and trials that we do not see the needs of others around us. Often in our search for contentment we forget that happiness is like a butterfly. If we try to catch the butterfly, it flies away. But when we busy ourselves with doing other tasks, the butterfly of happiness comes and lands on our shoulders. When we help others, we will find that our troubles disappear and delight lands in our life. The great Dr. Albert Schweitzer said, "One thing I know; the only ones among you who will be really happy are those who will have sought and found how to serve." We can serve by giving our money, time, and talents.

I am reminded of Jesus's words when He said, "It is more blessed to give than to receive" (Acts 20:35 NIV). How are you doing in your giving and serving leadership role?

Giving follows the law of sowing. A farmer sows seed into the soil.

In due time the seeds blossom, produce fruit, and feed many people (including the farmer). What can we learn from the farmer? We can't reap until we sow, nor will we experience the joy of giving until we do it. The seeds require time to germinate. We can't dig up the seeds every other day to see how they are growing. We may not see immediate results from our giving, but over time the seeds will bear fruit. The more seeds we sow, the more fruit will be produced. The more we develop the habit of giving and serving, the more others will be helped.

Years ago I saw a movie entitled *The Family Who Changed the World*. The story line revolved around the concept that the only world you can change is the one you live in. As you change the world you live in, you begin to affect the world at large.

Edward Kimball was a man who changed his world. He never became rich or famous. He not only gave his money to help others, but he also gave his time and service and faithfully taught Sunday school in a church in Boston.

Attending Edward's Sunday school class was a 17-year-old young man who had never personally received Christ as his Savior. This burdened the teacher's heart. Edward spent time with the young man and eventually led him to the Lord. Very few people remember the name Edward Kimball, but many people remember the name of the young man. His name was Dwight L. Moody. He later founded the Moody Bible Institute in Chicago. He had a great Christian impact in the United States and internationally.

Several years ago a movement started that encouraged "Random Acts of Kindness." The concept was designed to encourage us to think of others rather than of ourselves. These acts of kindness were designed to surprise the receiver. The act could take on almost any form, including leaving a larger than normal tip to a hardworking waitress or waiter, mowing someone's lawn, and babysitting.

I heard of one man who had been upgraded to first class on an airplane flight. As he was waiting to board the plane, he noticed a young mother with a small child. She looked very tired and worn out. He approached her and traded his first-class seat for her economy seat.

In your leadership role try to find someone or several people you can encourage. Can you lighten someone's burden today? Is it time to turn from looking at your trials and think of others instead? Ask God to open your eyes to the needs of others. Ask Him to give you a creative spirit to display His love through you. Jesus said, you are the light of the world.

> You are the light of the world. A town built on a hill cannot be hidden. Neither do people light a lamp and put it under a bowl. Instead they put it on its stand, and it gives light to everyone in the house. In the same way, let your light shine before others, that they may see your good deeds and glorify your Father in heaven (Matthew 5:14-16 NIV).

Dear Lord,

It's so easy to get lost in the forest of life's problems and forget about other people's needs. Help me to first see the needs of my family, since it is so easy to pass over their frustrations and struggles. Then, God, please open my eyes to see others and their personal battles. I want to be an encourager to the burdened. Help me reach out to others in the same way Christ reached out to me. May I look through Your eyes with Your love and endeavor to help others. Give me an expanded vision of the world around me. Help me to become a world changer.

Amen

LEADERSHIP SUCCESS

I expect to pass through life but once. If, therefore, there be any kindness I can show, or any good thing I can do to any fellow being, let me do it now, for I shall not pass this way again.

~ WILLIAM PENN

THE LIFE CYCLE
OF EVERY
ORGANIZATION

28

Ready to Change, Ready to Adapt

The reason most people never reach their goals is that they don't define them, learn about them, or even seriously consider them as believable or achievable. Winners can tell you where they are going, what they plan to do along the way, and who will be sharing the adventure with them.

~ DENIS WAITLEY

I'm sure you've heard it said that there are only two things that are for sure: death and taxes. You might consider another thing that's for sure...the human life cycle.

Individual Life Cycle

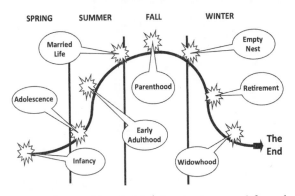

We all enter the world as babies, beginning our life cycle. This is followed by adolescence and early adulthood—and, for some, college years. For most people the next important events are marriage and parenthood. Granted, some remain single for various reasons. Those who have children will eventually go through the empty nest period when their children leave home, although today many children are returning for financial reasons. Then comes retirement, and some experience widowhood.

For most of our life cycle, we do pay taxes, but at some point we all will experience the end of our time on earth. The human life cycle has been likened to the seasons of the year: spring, summer, fall, and winter. All people live through various seasons or stages of life.

There is a similar life cycle that applies to organizations and even countries of the world. It's referred to as the Organizational Life Cycle.

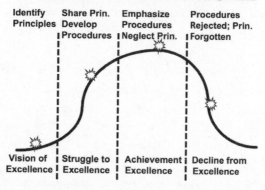

Organizations and nations have a beginning, and certain individuals arise as leaders. These leaders have some vision of greatness they would like to see accomplished for their group or nation. This vision is usually shared with others who desire to see the same things achieved. When about 5 percent of any group agree upon a vision and direction, their goal begins to generate heat and energy. Other people outside the original group begin to notice the passion, excitement, and energy created. This observation produces a desire to join in, becoming part of the movement. This is where leading through principles comes into play.

The vision of excellence is a time when individuals spend long hours, high dedication, and personal sacrifice for the desired vision or goal. They are driven by inspiration and often with little remuneration. In the Declaration of Independence, and later The Federalist Papers, the founders of America envisioned a unique land where all people could enjoy freedom to exercise what they believed were God-given rights. They defined and explained many important principles of this envisioned ideal state. They believed that among the most important principles are: (1) The Rule of Law, (2) Limited Government, and (3) Civic Virtue.

The Continental Army under the leadership of George Washington is an example. You may remember that Washington served without compensation during the Revolutionary War. The soldiers ranged in age from 16 to 50 years of age, with most in their twenties. They ate rotten food, experienced long marches, and wore poor clothing. It was said that you could trace the movement of Washington's army by the blood in the snow from the men who did not have shoes to wear. At Valley Forge, Washington lost 2,500 men during the winter. Their shelters were inadequate, and the men suffered from cold, damp quarters, typhoid, smallpox, dysentery, pneumonia, and malnutrition.

Why do you think they did this? Why would they follow Washington? They did it because of a vision of greatness that was bigger than their present circumstances. They had bought into the principles forming the foundation of this new country.

If you were to ask most Christians today to list their top three priorities, they might respond, "I put God first, my family second, and the nation last." If you were to ask the same question of the Revolutionary soldiers and the Founding Fathers, their reply would be different. They would say, "I put God first, the nation second, and my family last." They knew that if their nation lost its freedom, their families would be greatly affected. They fought for their families by fighting for the nation.

During the war years many people criticized Washington for his inability to win victories and advance the war. In his frustration Washington replied to his detractors:

> I can assure those Gentlemen that it is a much easier and
> less distressing thing to draw remonstrances [strong reasons

or facts against something complained of or opposed] in a comfortable room by a good fire side than to occupy a cold bleak hill and sleep under frost and Snow without Clothes or Blankets; however, although they seem to have little feeling for the naked, and distressed Soldier, I feel super-abundantly for them, and from my Soul pity those miseries, [which], it is neither in my power to relieve or prevent.

As a movement grows, more and more people are drawn in. When about 15 percent of the group or nation becomes followers, the movement develops its own momentum. That energy becomes difficult to slow down and may, in fact, be unstoppable.

This 5 to 15 percent principle works both positively and negatively. If the movement is humanitarian, such as to feed the hungry or to eliminate a disease like AIDS, the societal response is positive. If, however, the movement is designed to destroy a race of people through genocide or to enlarge a drug cartel, the murderers and drug lords receive a negative response.

For any movement to be truly great and positive for mankind, it needs to be based on solid principles. These principles become the foundation upon which character is developed. From character, or the lack of character, behavior is displayed.

Principle ➡ Character ➡ Behavior

Even though we may not always be aware, God is intimately involved with each of our life cycles. He engages with us throughout every stage of our lives.

> For You formed my innermost parts;
> You knit me [together] in my mother's womb.
> I will give thanks *and* praise to You, for I am fearfully and wonderfully made;
> Wonderful are Your works,
> And my soul knows it very well.
> My frame was not hidden from You,
> When I was being formed in secret,

And intricately *and* skillfully formed [as if embroidered with many colors] in the depths of the earth.
Your eyes have seen my unformed substance;
And in Your book were all written
The days that were appointed *for me*,
When as yet there was not one of them [even taking shape].
How precious also are Your thoughts to me, O God!
How vast is the sum of them! (Psalm 139:13-17).

Dear Lord,

As I begin to consider my own life cycle, please give me insight as to how You have been working in my circumstances from childhood to adulthood. As I think about the life cycle of the organization I work with, help me to understand its various stages of development. I want to be an effective leader regardless of which stage it's presently in. I want my life to glorify You at home, at work, or wherever You may lead me. I look forward to walking into the future, knowing You are not caught off guard by anything that will happen. I'm trusting in You to give me direction.

Amen

LEADERSHIP SUCCESS

I have learned that faith means trusting in advance what will only make sense in reverse.

~ PHILIP YANCEY

29

Stage One:
A Vision of Excellence

All the world's a stage, and all the men and women merely players:
they have their exits and their entrances; and one man in his
time plays many parts, his acts being seven ages.

~ WILLIAM SHAKESPEARE

The first stage of organizational leadership involves a "Vision of Excellence." People often ask, "Where does a vision for excellence come from?" It usually comes from one individual and not a committee of people. "What's driving this individual to want to pursue excellence?" The driving force often has its foundation in dysfunction. Something is wrong. Something is not working well. Something is causing trouble. Something has hurt individuals or the company. The individual with a vision says, "There must be a better way to do this. We're going to be in trouble if we keep going down this path. We need to change."

At this point of discouragement or frustration, the individual with a vision for excellence (or, a better way) begins to talk to other people about their concern. As a small group of people discuss the "Vision for Excellence," more creative ideas and suggestions are added to the vision. The rough vision begins to take practical form and is polished by the group. This is the beginning of action and change. As this group grows to about 5 percent of the organization, other people take notice, become interested, and commit to the vision.

As the vision takes form, a visionary (entrepreneurial) leader, begins to emerge and is trusted by the group. The leader moves the group to establish a mission based on principles that everyone can agree upon.

The energy and excitement of the leader and the group soon create a passionate commitment to the mission.

Developing a vision is not an easy task. It involves the wisdom and counsel of many people who contribute. The vision must be practical. It has to be a worthy enough challenge to draw people in and for  them to put forth energy toward the goal. It involves setting a standard for excellence that everyone identifies with and will support. The vision must not be complex. It needs to be easy to understand and clear enough to inspire enthusiasm and commitment.

Henry Ford gives an example of a clear and understandable vision in the following statement when he says, "I will build a motor car for the great multitude...The horse will have disappeared from our highways, the automobile will be taken for granted."

The beginning stages usually lack a formal organizational structure for the vision. There are few routines that have been established, and system flow is loose. Everyone is immersed in the project, mission, or goal. There's little hierarchy—all are too concerned about the mission rather than who's the boss.

> Sooner or later, all the thinking and planning
> has to degenerate to work.
>
> ~ PETER F. DRUCKER

The atmosphere is one of fun, excitement, and challenge. Action and production are driving forces. Passion and high energy carry the people through long hours and personal sacrifice. Paid staff and volunteers join in something that's bigger than a single individual. Financial rewards are usually very low at the beginning, and often the cash flow is low or lacking. Word of mouth enjoyment attracts others to join in the loosely organized group. The organization tends to be flatline rather than top-down leadership.

Where is your organization in the life cycle? What changes do you need to make as a leader?

> Let us not grow weary *or* become discouraged in doing good, for at the proper time we will reap, if we do not give in (Galatians 6:9).

Dear Lord,

Help me to be a practical, visionary type of leader. Give me the wisdom to identify principles that will guide and direct the vision. Give me the excitement and enthusiasm to challenge the people I lead toward a mission that creates energy and motivation. Help me to be open to suggestions that will make our vision attractive and more polished. Help me to be more concerned about the well-being of the people I lead rather than worrying about my acceptance as a leader. I'm looking forward with anticipation to what You are going to do in the days ahead. Help me to realize that You're more concerned about the future than I could ever be.

Amen

LEADERSHIP SUCCESS

This is the real secret of life—to be completely engaged with what you are doing in the here and now. And instead of calling it work, realize it is play.

~ ALAN WATTS

30

Stage Two:
The Struggle for Excellence

*Life is like a game of chess. To win you have to make a move.
Knowing which move to make comes with insight and knowledge
and by learning the lessons that are accumulated along the way.
We become each and every piece within this game called life.*

~ ALLAN RUFUS

The second stage of organizational leadership involves a "Struggle to Excellence."

As the organization begins to grow, it encounters growing pains. Authority has to be delegated and divided, and leaders get added. Management systems become a necessity. Various departments are created, and teams are formed. Rather than people being generalists, their jobs

Organizational Life Cycle

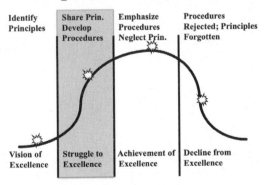

| Identify Principles | Share Prin. Develop Procedures | Emphasize Procedures Neglect Prin. | Procedures Rejected; Principles Forgotten |

| Vision of Excellence | Struggle to Excellence | Achievement of Excellence | Decline from Excellence |

become more technical and specialized. Decisions are passed down to committees. Job descriptions are implemented so people do not step on each other's feet. Staff meetings seem to last longer. The company experiences culture change.

The need for open communication and clarification becomes essential. Staff newsletters are formulated. Conflicts between people, schedules, and methods arise. Departments, leaders, and line workers tend to feel threatened and/or imposed upon. Discomfort, misunderstanding, and frustration grow. Occasional change turns into continual change, and adjustment becomes complex.

To keep up with rapid production, tracking systems are created. Paperwork, forms, and reporting systems increase dramatically. The expansion of documentation begins to be resented by overworked staff.

Training and retraining become a necessity to remain on the cutting edge of competition. The company constantly faces the struggle between quantity and quality. The organization needs to adapt to change or face stagnation and financial downturn. Research and innovation expand to meet growing pressure.

In the struggle for excellence, team-building leadership is essential. The ability to analyze and plan for the future is of prime importance. The growth in the struggle for excellence is often erratic and unstable because of the constant changes and adjustments. The leader needs not only to be highly creative, adaptive, and encouraging...but they also need to lead with good, effective, and quick decision-making. They need to bring balance and a steady hand during unsteady growth.

The leader must increase his or her skills in conflict resolution and problem-solving. They need to watch for staff burnout and overwork. To survive well they need to adapt and be able to live with and adjust to continual change. They need to be able to juggle multiple priorities.

- Advertising and Marketing
- Big Challenges

- Board of Directors
- Computer Systems
- Creation of Financial Reports
- Criticism and Dissatisfaction
- Discontent and Dismay
- Fund-raising Efforts
- Heavier Workload
- Making Peace with the Unknown
- Research and Development
- Risk Taking

Where is your organization in the life cycle? What leadership changes do you need to make at this time?

> Trust [rely on and have confidence] in the LORD and do good;
> Dwell in the land and feed [securely] on His faithfulness.
> Delight yourself in the LORD,
> And He will give you the desires *and* petitions of your heart.
> Commit your way to the LORD;
> Trust in Him also and He will do it.
> He will make your righteousness [your pursuit of right standing with God] like the light,
> And your judgment like [the shining of] the noonday [sun].
> Be still before the LORD; wait patiently for Him *and* entrust yourself to Him;
> Do not fret (whine, agonize) because of him who prospers in his way...
> Do not fret; *it leads* only to evil.
> For those who do evil will be cut off,
> But those who wait for the LORD, they will inherit the land...

But the humble will [at last] inherit the land
And will delight themselves in abundant prosperity *and*
    peace (Psalm 37:3-9,11).

Dear Lord,

Help me to be a visionary and encouraging leader that can be focused on and concerned about principles and mission. Help me to lead in such a way that our company becomes organized well and focused on positive goals. Help me to be more concerned as to why we do what we are doing rather than how we are doing it. Help me to be alert to the needs of those who work under me. Help me not to let them get stressed, overworked, and out of balance. Help me to eliminate unnecessary paperwork and fruitless projects. Give me direction for good, effective, and quick decision-making. Help me to be aware of issues that might cause conflict and give me the skills to deal with it when it occurs. Thank for what You're going to do.

Amen

LEADERSHIP SUCCESS

Go as far as you can see; when you get there, you'll be able to see farther.

~ J.P. MORGAN

31

Stage Three:
Achieving Excellence

Golf is the closest game to the game we call life. You
get bad breaks from good shots. You get good breaks
from bad shots...but you have to play the ball.

~ BOBBY JONES

The third stage of organizational leadership involves an "Achievement of Excellence."

Sometimes an organization is so focused on growth, expansion, and quality that they leadership is not aware they've achieved excellence. The achievement sort of sneaks up, surprising them. The reality of success takes a little time to sink in.

There are three clear signs that a company or organization is succeeding:

1. They have a positive reputation and are well received by the general public. The public is happy and satisfied with the product or the service.

2. They are appreciated and respected by other organizations in the same business field. The approval of peers who make a similar product or provide the same service is a tremendous compliment.

3. Others consult them, inquiring how they have achieved such a positive reputation. This means their influence is spreading and can have a positive impact with individuals, society, and a culture.

Achievement of excellence means the organization has remained true and steady to the foundational principles and mission they've chosen. It also means the organization has inspired its employees to become living examples of the mission.

Leadership in this type of organization has been able to attract followers who are inspired and motivated to support the mission and the leader. A creative and visionary leader can understand and focus both on the details of the operation and on big picture issues.

A successful organization indicates that a dedicated leader has the ability and track record to make difficult decisions and be held accountable for his or her choices. It means the leader also has been willing to take calculated risks and set the direction for the company or organization.

To achieve excellence requires strategic planning, problem-solving, and teamwork. Research and development are part of excellence, along with the desire to continually improve the product or service.

But within the positive seeds of improvement and excellence come seeds that are dangerous and harmful. The seeds of pride, the seeds of self-satisfaction, and the seeds of laziness and complacency are lurking. There are also seeds of uncertainty. Questions arise, such as "Where do we go from here?" and "Do we need to establish a new mission or direction?"

With the addition of new employees who do not know the history of the organization come the winds of change—for change's sake. Old standards are blown out the window. There's a tendency to forget why things were first done. Often new people reinvent the wheel—repeatedly.

Some very successful organizations begin to forget the founding principles...and even stray from their original mission. Rather than depending on and stressing principles, they begin to emphasize procedures. *How* the organization does things becomes more important than *why*. Good examples include Harvard, Yale, Dartmouth, and

Cambridge Universities. They were all founded with a Christian mission. Today they are far removed from their original founding principles. In fact, it's estimated that 106 out of 108 of the first colleges established in America were Christian colleges.

Organizational Life Cycle

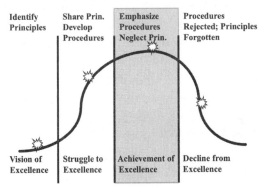

| Identify Principles | Share Prin. Develop Procedures | Emphasize Procedures Neglect Prin. | Procedures Rejected; Principles Forgotten |

| Vision of Excellence | Struggle to Excellence | Achievement of Excellence | Decline from Excellence |

To stay in the area of "Achievement of Excellence," the organization needs to return to the founding principles and mission of the company. It needs to establish a new life cycle that begins to clean up company trash (unnecessary details and programs) and develop a new struggle for excellence. This process is best reviewed about every five to seven years.

Where is your organization in the life cycle? What leadership changes do you need to make at this time?

> Let the peace of Christ [the inner calm of one who walks daily with Him] be the controlling factor in your hearts [deciding and settling questions that arise]. To this *peace* indeed you were called as members in one body [of believers]. And be thankful [to God always] Let the [spoken] word of Christ have its home within you [dwelling in your heart and mind—permeating every aspect of your being] as you teach [spiritual things] and admonish *and* train one another with all wisdom, singing psalms and hymns and spiritual songs with thankfulness in your hearts to God. Whatever you do [no matter what it is] in word or deed, do

everything in the name of the Lord Jesus [and in dependence on Him], giving thanks to God the Father through Him (Colossians 3:15-17).

Dear Lord,

Help me to be aware of all the excellence You provide. Teach me to hold fast to the mission and to encourage others to do the same thing. Give me direction in making difficult decisions that could affect our organization dramatically. Give me the faith to trust You and risk great things for You. Alert me to the dangerous seeds of pride, laziness, and complacency. Please don't let me be caught in those sins. Help me to teach the "story pole" of history to those under my leadership. Help us not to reinvent the wheel or pursue fruitless pathways. Help me to lead our team to create a new life cycle in the pursuit of excellence.

Amen

LEADERSHIP SUCCESS

If God would grant us the vision, the word *sacrifice* would disappear from our lips and thoughts; we would hate the things that seem now so dear to us; our lives would suddenly be too short, we would despise time-robbing distractions and charge the enemy with all our energies in the name of Christ.

~NATE SAINT

32

Stage Four:
Coping with the Challenges

Life is like a piano.
What you get out of it depends on how you play it.

~ Tom Lehrer

The fourth stage of organizational leadership involves a "Decline from Excellence."

The decline from excellence usually doesn't happen rapidly. It often begins with changes in leadership. For some reason new leaders feel compelled to make changes in direction. Those changes begin to move away from the founding principles and even from various procedures that have been successful. These new directional changes are often made without consideration for the past and the advice of counselors or boards of directors.

Sometimes leaders who have helped the organization or company to the stage of "Achievement of Excellence" move into a dangerous state of mind. They're a little tired from all the hard work and feel they deserve a rest. They begin to slack off their vision and drive. They think they're entitled to special perks, such as not spending a full eight or more hours on the job. They start to ignore tasks and duties that had brought them to success.

Sometimes the decline begins when the organization has grown larger than the leader's abilities to handle it. The person may be good, loyal, and moral but has moved into what's called the Peter Principle. This principle suggests that the individual has risen to their level of incompetence. They no longer have the necessary skills or knowledge needed for the task at hand. And since they are lacking in skills and knowledge, they remain in a position where they begin to frustrate and hinder everyone who works for them.

This type of leader may begin to sense their inadequacies and feel fearful and threatened. They may begin to withdraw from people and situations that are difficult to deal with. Decision-making becomes a scary task. They start to disappear from those who work for them. Staff find it difficult to meet with the leader, who is never available for appointments or simply seems to disappear. Their team has no idea where the leader is and wonders what happened. Rumors then emerge: How can the leader move from place to place and no one sees them? Are there secret tunnels underground where they travel from one spot to another?

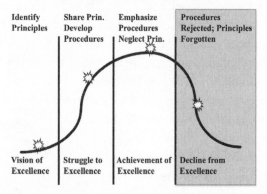

Organizational Life Cycle

Identify Principles	Share Prin. Develop Procedures	Emphasize Procedures Neglect Prin.	Procedures Rejected; Principles Forgotten
Vision of Excellence	Struggle to Excellence	Achievement of Excellence	Decline from Excellence

Leadership changes also occur during the "Achievement of Excellence." These changes touch off unfortunate concepts or philosophies of leadership. One of those is a change of job description for the leader. During the "Achievement of Excellence," the leader is often a very hands-on type of personality. They seem to have a working knowledge of all aspects of the company even though they do not personally attend to the details of each job.

When a new leader is chosen, sometimes a new philosophy accompanies them. They, or their board of directors, think the new leader does not need to be hands-on as past leaders have been. The organization is functioning well, and the new leader can rise to a higher level. They can now lead from a "thirty-thousand-foot level" where they see the big picture and not lowly details. The staff under them can attend to all the minor issues.

This sounds good at first glance. The leader certainly needs to have the big picture of what's going on. The danger, though, lies in what happens when things begin to fall apart at a lower level. Who deals with or oversees those problems? The truth is, the buck cannot be passed. The leader is still responsible and accountable for everything that happens.

Is there a final decision maker in the company? Of course! That's why many people don't want to be a leader. They may desire the title of leader but don't want the responsibility and accountability. When the leader is not hands-on, or when they don't at least understand the aspects of all jobs, how can they make effective decisions for their organization? This new philosophy of leadership has within it the seeds of a decline from excellence. This is something to seriously consider. Listed below are some of the signs of possible decline from excellence.

- Accountants rule decisions
- Becoming a caretaker
- Board over control
- Communication lacking
- Defensive organization
- Demands for service decline
- Everyone seems tired
- Key staff members leave
- Lazy and fat
- Leader not present
- Leader not right fit

- Little direction
- Living in the past
- Momentum slows
- No succession plan
- Organization imploding
- Organization is spotty
- Ostentatious facilities
- Paperwork rises
- Pride and arrogance
- Principles forgotten
- Procedures rejected
- Seems out of touch
- Staff morale drops
- Stagnation
- Stops taking risks
- Support drops off
- Uncertain vision
- Vision becomes fuzzy
- Well-oiled social club

Where is your organization in the life cycle? What changes do you need to make at this time as a leader?

Today, and every day, deliver more than you are getting paid to do.
The victory of success will be half won when you learn the secret
of putting out more than is expected in all that you do.
Make yourself so valuable in your work
that eventually you will become indispensable.
Exercise your privilege to go the extra mile,
and enjoy all the rewards you receive.
You deserve them!

~ OG MANDINO

So then, let us [who minister] be regarded as servants of Christ and stewards (trustees, administrators) of the mysteries of God [that He chooses to reveal]. In this case, moreover, it is required [as essential and demanded] of stewards that one be found faithful *and* trustworthy (1 Corinthians 4:1-2).

Dear Lord,

It is an awesome thought to ponder a decline from excellence. Please alert me to any signs of decline that I need to address. I don't want to be a leader who shirks responsibilities. Please help me to evaluate my leadership, my vision, and my accountability. Help me in my leadership to be a protector of those who work under me and of the organization I work for. Please give me renewed energy and vision to lead into the future.

Amen

LEADERSHIP SUCCESS

Excellence is an art won by training and habituation. We do not act rightly because we have virtue or excellence, but we rather have those because we have acted rightly. We are what we repeatedly do. Excellence, then, is not an act but a habit.

~ ARISTOTLE

TOOLS FOR EVERY LEADER

Leadership Resources

In the following pages you will find numerous thoughts related to leadership. These various pages were collected over many years. Some bear the name of the author. Many will not list the author's name because I do not know who originally wrote them or where they came from. The words have been included in this book as possible ideas that could benefit you in your leadership position. I hope you will enjoy them as much as I have. Thank you to all the authors even though we do not know who you are.

33

What Is a Leader?

As nearly everyone knows, a leader has practically nothing to do except:

decide what is to be done; tell somebody to do it; listen to reasons why it should not be done or why it should be done in a different way; follow up to see if the thing has been done; discover that it has not; inquire why; listen to excuses from the person who should have done it; follow up again to see if the thing has been done, only to discover that it has been done incorrectly; point out how it should have been done; conclude that as long as it has been done, it may as well be left where it is; wonder if it is not time to get rid of a person who cannot do a thing right; reflect that the person probably has a spouse and a large family, and any successor would be just as bad—or maybe worse; consider how much simpler and better matters would be now if he had done it himself in the first place; reflect sadly that he could have done it right in 20 minutes and, as things turned out, he has had to spend two days to find out why it has taken three weeks for somebody else to do it wrong.

34

Leadership Potential

Adapted from George Barna and used by permission

1. Do I have effective communication skills?   Yes No
2. Can I identify, articulate, and cast vision?   Yes No
3. Do I have the ability to motivate people?   Yes No
4. Do I have the ability to coach and develop people?   Yes No
5. Do I process and synthesize information well?   Yes No
6. Do I have the ability to persuade people?   Yes No
7. Do I do well at initiating strategic action?   Yes No
8. Do I find myself engaging in strategic thinking?   Yes No
9. Do I deliberately attempt to resolve conflict?   Yes No
10. Do I work at developing resources?   Yes No
11. Can I delegate authority and responsibility?   Yes No
12. Do I help to reinforce commitment from people?   Yes No
13. Do I celebrate successes with people?   Yes No
14. Do I have good decision-making skills?   Yes No
15. Am I good at team building?   Yes No
16. Do I take time in the evaluation of people, programs, and activities?   Yes No
17. Do I create a positive corporate culture?   Yes No
18. Do I have the ability to maintain focus and set priorities?   Yes No
19. Do I hold people to be accountable?   Yes No

20. Am I aware of opportunities for influence?   Yes No

21. Do I have the ability to manage other key leaders?   Yes No

22. Am I a model of spiritual disciplines?   Yes No

23. Do I follow God's plans and principles?   Yes No

24. Do I have people working under me who
    see me as a leader?   Yes No

25. Do the people under me follow me willingly?   Yes No

How do you match up? Are there any areas that need to be improved in your life? What is your plan to sharpen your skills? If in the process of answering these questions you were uncomfortable or wished that there was a 1-10 grading scale, it might be good for you to reevaluate and determine if leadership is in your skill set. All of the above competencies are essential in a leadership role.

MAJOR LEADERSHIP QUESTION

Do You have a Readiness for Responsibility?

YES NO

35

An Attitude Checklist

Please read the following questions and rate your present attitude on a scale of 1 to 10. If you circle a 1 you would be saying that your attitude is low or negative. If you circle a 10 you would be saying your attitude is high or very positive. Rate your *honest* feelings about your attitude at this time in your life.

Negative (Low)/Positive (High)

1. My employer would rate my job
performance and attitude as a   1 2 3 4 5 6 7 8 9 10

2. The fellow workers at my job or my school
friends would rate me with an attitude of   1 2 3 4 5 6 7 8 9 10

3. My family, who really knows me, would say
that my attitude at home would deserve a   1 2 3 4 5 6 7 8 9 10

4. The way I respond to, or get along with, friends
and strangers would give me a rating of   1 2 3 4 5 6 7 8 9 10

5. The way I deal with daily frustrations, along
with my patience and tolerance level would
give me a number   1 2 3 4 5 6 7 8 9 10

6. The amount of care, concern, and sensitivity
that I show to others would give a rating of   1 2 3 4 5 6 7 8 9 10

7. My happiness level and the sense of humor
I display would give me a number   1 2 3 4 5 6 7 8 9 10

8. My enthusiasm toward life and my work at
   this period would register the rating of   1 2 3 4 5 6 7 8 9 10

9. My overall view of my attitude at this time
   would get a realistic rating of   1 2 3 4 5 6 7 8 9 10

10. If God were to rate my present attitude,
    I think He would give me a number   1 2 3 4 5 6 7 8 9 10

A score of 90 or above	Great attitude—pass it on
A score of 70 to 90	A few minor adjustments suggested
A score of 50 to 70	Major adjustments are recommended
A score of 50 or below	Time for a complete overhaul

When a man is gloomy, everything seems to go wrong; when he is cheerful, everything seems right! (Proverbs 15:15 TLB).

36

Gut Check: Evaluating Negative Attitudes

How do you deal with negative attitudes in the workplace? You may be called upon as a leader to deal with a troublesome employee in need of correction, discipline, or possibly firing. How do you document the behavior that needs to be corrected?

Problems in the areas of being late to work, stealing from the employer, or fighting on the job are easy to document. What's difficult is disciplining employees when it comes to a poor attitude.

How do you document a negative attitude? It's so subjective. For this reason, the following form was designed to help clarify and make objective the meaning of attitude in terms of word content, tone of voice, and nonverbal behavior. This form also can be useful in helping to identify conflict in attitude.

The employee with a negative attitude often does not see himself or herself as having any problems. When confronted, the individual might easily reply, "What do you mean when you say I've got a negative, hostile, or bad attitude?" What do you say in response? How can you help the employee become aware of their behavior?

This is a subjective evaluation and difficult to document, but nevertheless it is just as real. It involves the primary focus on how fellow workers and/or supervisors feel about, and whether they can work in harmony with, the evaluated individual.

Attitude is a consistent state of mind or feeling that,
over a period of time, manifests itself through the content of words,
tone of voice, and nonverbal behavior.

Attitude in Performing the Actual Work and the Corresponding Interpersonal Relationships Involved

CONTENT OF WORDS	TONE OF VOICE	NONVERBAL BEHAVIOR
☐ Put-down humor	☐ Talking down to	☐ Little eye contact
☐ Pessimistic	☐ Mimicking	☐ Walking away
☐ Angry	☐ Whining	☐ Ignoring
☐ Hostile	☐ Argumentative	☐ Hand and finger signs
☐ Rude	☐ Defensive	☐ Silent; angry stare
☐ Sarcastic	☐ Accusing	☐ Gritting of teeth
☐ Lying	☐ Yelling	☐ Making faces
☐ Bitter	☐ Attacking	☐ Throwing things
☐ Negative	☐ Grumpy	☐ Folding arms
☐ Gossip	☐ Grouchy	☐ Pouting
☐ Slander	☐ Impatient	☐ Tears
☐ Divisive	☐ Angry; cross	☐ Yawning
☐ Critical	☐ Testy; catty	☐ Raised eyebrows
☐ Irritated	☐ Sighs; grunts	☐ Frowns
☐ Spiteful	☐ Exasperated	☐ Angry looks

Look at the three categories.
Check all that apply and illustrate attitude problems.

37

Workplace Values

Look over the various values listed below. Rate them with one of the following: A—B—C—D—E. Determine which values need to be worked on and enhanced in your organization.

A—Always Valued
B—Often Valued
C—Sometimes Valued
D—Seldom Valued
E—Least Valued

_____ **Achievement**—Successful completion of visible tasks or projects

_____ **Advancement**—Getting ahead; ambitious; aspiring to higher levels

_____ **Adventure**—challenging; risk-taking; testing limits

_____ **Aesthetic**—Desire for beauty; artistic

_____ **Appearance**—Looking good; dressing well; keeping fit

_____ **Authority**—Having the power to direct events; making things happen

_____ **Belonging**—Being connected to and liked by others

_____ **Challenge**—Testing physical limits, strength, speed, and agility

_____ **Communication**—Open dialogue; exchange of views

_____ **Community**—Living where neighbors are close and involved

_____ **Competence**—Being good at what I do; capable; effective

_____ **Competition**—Winning; doing the best I can alongside others

_____ **Consensus**—Making decisions everyone can live with

_____ **Courageous**—Standing up for my beliefs; overcoming fear

_____ **Creativity**—Finding new ways to do things; innovative

_____ **Diplomacy**—Finding common ground with difficult people and situations

_____ **Fairness**—Similar opportunity; respecting everyone's rights

_____ **Family**—Taking care of and spending time with loved ones

_____ **Forgiveness**—Able to pardon others and let go of hurt

_____ **Friendship**—Close companionship; ongoing relationships

_____ **Health**—Maintaining and enhancing physical well-being

_____ **Helping**—Taking care of others and doing what they need

_____ **Honesty**—Sincere; open; truthful

_____ **Inner Harmony**—Freedom from inner conflict; integrated; whole

_____ **Integrity**—Acting in line with my talk and beliefs

_____ **Intellectual**—Being regarded as an expert; a person who knows

_____ **Intimacy**—Deep; emotional; spiritual connection

_____ **Knowledge**—Seeking intellectual stimulation, new ideas, truth, and understanding

_____ **Neatness**—Tidy; orderly; clean

_____ **Peace**—End of war; nonviolent conflict resolution

_____ **Perseverance**—Pushing through to the end; completing tasks

_____ **Personal Growth**—Continual learning; development of new skills; self-awareness

_____ **Play**—Fun; lightness; spontaneity

_____ **Pleasure**—Personal satisfaction; enjoyment; delight

_____ **Power**—Control over decision-making, projects, and movement of people

_____ **Prosperity**—Flourishing; well-off; affording what I want

_____ **Rationality**—Consistent; logical; clear reasoning; unemotional

_____ **Recognition**—Getting noticed for effective efforts

_____ **Respectful**—Showing consideration; regarding with honor

_____ **Security**—Freedom from worry; safe; risk free

_____ **Self-acceptance**—Self-respect; self-esteem

_____ **Self-control**—Self-disciplined; restrained

_____ **Spiritual Growth**—Relationship to and with God

_____ **Stability**—Certainty; predictability

_____ **Teamwork**—Cooperating with others toward a common goal

_____ **Tolerance**—Respectful of others

_____ **Tradition**—Respecting the way things have always been done

The 80/20 Principle

The 80/20 Principle (also called the Pareto Principle) was first introduced by Vilfredo Pareto. He was an Italian economist who, in 1896, first published the concept. It suggests that for many of life's events, 80 percent of the effects come from, or are produced by, 20 percent of the causes.

Examples include:

80 percent of problems can be attributed to 20 percent of causes.

80 percent of a company's profits come from 20 percent of its customers.

80 percent of complaints are generated by 20 percent of the customers or churchgoers.

80 percent of a company's profits are created by 20 percent of the time its staff spend.

80 percent of business sales come from 20 percent of its products.

80 percent of an organization's sales are made by 20 percent of its sales staff.

80 percent of computer crashes are caused by 20 percent of the most reported bugs.

80 percent of health care resources are used by 20 percent of the patients.

80 percent of crimes are the result of 20 percent of the criminals.

80 percent of donated money comes from 20 percent of the givers.

80 percent of carpet wear occurs in 20 percent of the carpet area.

80 percent of time is spent in unprofitable areas; is 20 percent of time spent in profitable areas.

80 percent of happiness is experienced in 20 percent of life.

Where do you think we should spend most of our time?

The following Mood Signs indicate you may be working in the 80 percent task zone rather than in the 20 percent task zone.

Check the ones that apply to you:

- ☐ You dread going to meetings.
- ☐ You have feelings of detachment.
- ☐ You feel listless much of the time.
- ☐ You're always watching the clock.
- ☐ You're beginning to be late for meetings.
- ☐ You're beginning to experience boredom.
- ☐ You really do not like what you are doing.
- ☐ You find yourself more and more impatient.
- ☐ You put off returning phone calls and emails.
- ☐ You're having more and more escape feelings.
- ☐ You're finding yourself more and more forgetful.
- ☐ You find yourself taking more and more sick days.
- ☐ You're told by other people that you seem irritable.
- ☐ You're beginning to find yourself becoming depressed.

☐ You find yourself frequently working on tasks marked "urgent."

☐ You are involved in tasks that you are not usually good at doing.

☐ You feel like there's too much paperwork and unproductive business.

☐ You notice that projects, activities, and tasks are taking longer than you expected.

☐ You're working on tasks other people assign you but are not really invested in them.

Count the total number of boxes you checked:

1-5   Normal feelings

5-10   Some discomfort with tasks

11-15   Too many project stressors

16-20   Time for an overhaul

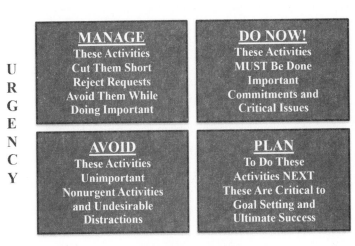

IMPORTANCE

39

Leading Versus Managing

On a percentage scale from 1 percent to 100 percent —How much of your thinking, energy, time, and interest is spent in Leading compared to Managing?

Leaders have the ability and capability to focus on and understand the big picture—the context of events and functions, the networking

LEADER									*MANAGER*
100%	80%	60%	40%	20%		20%	40%	60%	80%	100%

of ideas and circumstances, and the behaviors of people. Not only do they grasp how the past, present, and future interrelate, but they tend to move ideas, events, and people in a specific direction.

Managers frequently have a smaller circle of focus and tend to see parts and individual pieces and concentrate on them. They more often submit and surrender to the direction of others. They commonly wait for direction from above and usually do not generate or create new concepts and methods of accomplishment.

Thought to keep in mind: At times we all exercise leadership and other times we all do management tasks. The questions are: Which do you feel more comfortable doing? If you had a choice, which side feels more comfortable to you? Which side do you gravitate toward?

THE TENDENCY OF LEADERS	THE TENDENCY OF MANAGERS
Ideas	Facts
Broad	Narrow
Deep	Surface
Experiential	Rote
Active	Passive
Questions	Answers
Process	Content
Strategy	Tactics
Alternatives	Goals
Exploration	Prediction
Discovery	Dogma
Active	Reactive
Initiative	Direction
Whole brain	Left brain
Life	Job
Long term	Short term
Change	Stability
Content	Form
Flexible	Rigid
Risk	Rules
Synthesis	Thesis
Open	Closed
Imagination	Common sense

40

The Power of Delegation

Once upon a time there was a Little Red Hen who owned a wheat field.

"Who will help me harvest the wheat?" she asked.

"Not I," said the pig. "I don't know how."

"Not I," said the cow. "I'm too clumsy."

"Not I," said the dog. "I'm too busy with some other things."

So the Little Red Hen did it herself.

"Who will help me grind the wheat into flour?" she asked.

"Not I," said the pig. "That is another vocation in which I'm untrained."

"Not I," said the cow. "You could do it more efficiently."

"Not I," said the dog. "I'd love to, but I'm involved in some matters of greater urgency. Some other time, perhaps."

So the Little Red Hen did it herself.

"Who will help me make some bread?" asked the Little Red Hen.

"Not I," said the pig. "Nobody ever taught me how."

"Not I," said the cow. "You're more experienced and could do it in half the time."

"Not I," said the dog. "I've made some other plans for the afternoon. But I'll help you next time."

So the Little Red Hen did it herself.

That evening, when guests arrived for her big dinner party, the Little Red Hen had nothing to serve them except bread. She had been so busy doing work that could have been done by others that she had for-gotten to plan a main course, prepare a desert, or even get out the sil-verware. The evening was a disaster, and she lived unhappily ever after.

Moral: A good leader will find a way to involve
others to the extent of their ability.
To do the job yourself is the chicken way out.

41

Opening Dialogue

- What do you think I did or failed to do that contributed to the conflict?

- Can you give me a specific example?

- How did you feel when I did that?

- Can you tell me more about what bothered you that I did?

- What do you think you did or failed to do that contributed to the conflict?

- Would you like to know how that made me feel?

- What did you mean when you said...?

- Why does what I said create a problem for you?

- What is the worst part of what happened for you?

- Why don't you tell me about your experience, and I'll listen to you. Then I'll tell you about mine.

- I hope you can hear what I'm saying without getting upset or angry or confused. Will you let me know if what I say starts to bother you so I can communicate with you better?

- If you had it to do over again, what would you do differently? Why?

- Would you be willing to start over again right now and do it differently?

- What is most important to you in solving this problem?

- Can you think of any solutions that might be acceptable to both of us?

- What would it take for you to let go of this conflict and feel the issues have really been completely resolved?

- How would you like me to communicate with you in the future if there are any more problems? What should I say if I experience a problem?

- Would you be interested in hearing how I would like you to communicate with me in the future?

- What kind of relationship would you like to have with me?

- What can we do to make our next conversation go more smoothly?

- Is reconciliation even possible in our relationship? If so, what would need to be done to make reconciliation a reality?

42

Becoming Visionary

1. Some people never see it. (They are wanderers.)
2. Some people see it but never pursue it on their own. (They are followers.)
3. Some people see it and pursue it. (They are achievers.)
4. Some people see it and pursue it and help others to see it. (They are leaders.)

A Person With a Vision...	A Visionary Person...
talks little but does much.	does little but talks much.
draws strength from inner convictions.	draws strength from outward conditions.
continues when problems arise.	quits when the road becomes difficult.

What hinders a vision?

1. Limited Leaders
2. Concrete Thinkers
3. Dogmatic Talkers
4. Continual Losers
5. Satisfied Sitters
6. Tradition Lovers
7. Census Takers

8. Problem Perceivers

9. Self-Seekers

10. Failure Forecasters

Vision: A mental image produced by the imagination. It involves discernment, perception, and foresight. It is the ability to picture the future by creative thought and conceptualization. Vision is creating something out of nothing that ever existed before. Vision is a word painting.

Where there is no vision the people perish (Proverbs 29:18 KJV).

In Matthew Henry's Commentary, Henry suggests that the terms "the people perish" or "run wild" carry the following meanings:

1. The people are made naked and thereby are exposed to danger.

2. The people rebel.

3. The people are idle, or they play.

4. The people are scattered as sheep having no shepherd.

5. The people are destroyed for a lack of knowledge.

Vision comes in advance of any task well done.

~ JONATHAN SWIFT

The farther backward you can look,
The farther forward you are likely to see.

~ WINSTON CHURCHILL

Those who have most powerfully and permanently influenced
their generation have been "seers"...
people who have seen more and farther than others...
persons of faith, for faith is vision.
Vision involves foresight as well as insight.

A leader must be able to see the end results
of the policies and methods he or she advocates.
Responsible leadership always looks ahead
to see how policies will affect future generations.
Vision includes optimism and hope.
Vision leads to venture, and history is on the side
of venturesome faith.
Leaders take lessons from the past,
but never sacrifice the future for the sake of mere continuity.
People of vision gauge decisions on the future,
the story of the past cannot be rewritten.

~ J. OSWALD SANDERS

If God would grant us the vision,
the word "sacrifice" would disappear from our lips and thoughts.
We would hate the things that now seem dear to us,
our lives would suddenly be too short,
we would despise time robbing distractions,
and charge the enemy with all our energy in the name of Christ.

~ NATE SAINT

43

Changing Behavior

Have you ever had to make an important decision and needed help in the process? Have you wondered if the decision you had to make was right or wrong, good or bad, positive or negative, moral or immoral, or legal or illegal? The Behavior Box may help give you guidance.

Put the decision you must make into the Behavior Box, and then begin to ask questions. Is the decision okay on the *Natural* person's level? Will the decision be accepted on the *Social* person's level? Would the *Moral* person think the decision is acceptable? If God was the final judge on your decision, would He approve it?

For example, let's consider smoking. What would the natural person think? Perhaps: "Do whatever you want to do. It's your life and you answer to yourself."

The social person might have a question: "Should you think about other people? They might not be happy with your secondhand smoke. Many public places will not allow smoking. If you must smoke, do it outside."

The moral person might respond, "It's not a question of morality. You can be a moral person and still smoke. It might become a question more about your health."

When it comes to what God might think about your decision, it would be good to search the Bible for His answer. When the Bible is silent on some subjects, then what are you to do? Ask the following questions: Will the behavior in question help or hinder my witness and testimony? Will my behavior bring glory and honor to God, or dishonor? That's the deeper and harder question.

Now you have a real decision to make. To help you in the area of smoking, you can now pray a short prayer to God, saying, "Dear Lord, I'm going to light this cigarette and smoke it to Your honor and glory." Remember, smoking won't send you to Hell; it just makes you smell like you've been there. Anyway, you get the point. You must be very straightforward and honest as you seek to make important decisions.

> Whatever you do [no matter what it is] in word or deed, do everything in the name of the Lord Jesus [and in dependence on Him], giving thanks to God the Father through Him (Colossians 3:17).

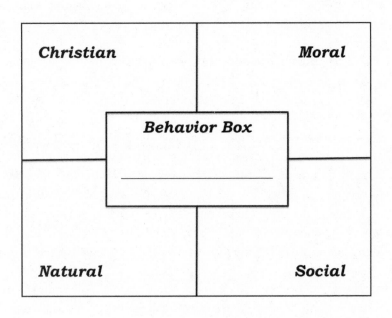

44

Tried and True Principles for Conflict Management and Problem Solving

Effective confrontation means telling another person the effect that his or her behavior has on you. The goal of confrontation is to get your own needs met without the other person becoming and remaining defensive.

Four-Part Confrontation Message

When someone does something specific that has had a concrete and tangible effect on your life, then it's important to send a four-part confrontation message. The goal of this message is to get the other to change his or her behavior, but in his or her own way. Confrontation is not the sending of solutions. It's the defense of one's own right in a nonjudgmental manner.

When you_____... (Nonjudgmentally describe the behavior.)

I feel_____... (Nonjudgmentally disclose your feelings.)

because_____... (State the concrete and tangible effect on you.)

I would like_____. (Share the behavior you would appreciate in the future.)

Hints

1. When describing behavior, be accurate and specific; keep the description as brief as possible, and avoid absolutes like "never," "always," and "every time."

2. When disclosing feelings, choose a word that accurately reflects the intensity of your emotion (i.e., if you're "angry," don't use the word "irritated" or "confused"); choose a word that is your real emotion. Avoid the use of words that are judgmental or hurtful to the other person with the intention to make them feel guilty.

3. When stating the concrete and tangible effect on you, try not to relate it to a "relationship problem." (That's more subjective.) It's better to mention it cost you money. It harms your possessions. It costs you extra time. It interferes with work effectiveness. It endangers your job, etc.

4. When sharing what you would like to see, be specific rather than general. Describe the behavior that would help the situation not to reoccur in the future. For example: "I would appreciate it if you would clean up your mess after making snacks for yourself."

Considerations for Delivering a Confrontation Message

1. Consider whether you have a right to confront.

2. Consider the concrete and tangible effect on you.

3. If possible, write out your message.

4. Weigh the likelihood of success. Is it worth it? How risky is it, even if it's worth it?

5. Roleplay it with someone, or at least rehearse it privately.

6. When you finally do confront, don't delay...get right to it.

7. Make sure your entire message is consistent.

8. Expect the other person to become defensive. Actively listen until the other's tension lowers. Then start over with your message and active listening.

9. Do not conclude your confrontation until the other buys into or owns his or her half of the problem and agrees to mutually problem-solve for a solution.

10. Mutually agree to follow up and evaluate the effectiveness of the solution.

If Your Four-Part Confrontation Message Fails:

1. Reexamine the message itself. You may have been judgmental, or there may have been no concrete and tangible effect mentioned.

2. You may have an inconsistent message. Your voice or body could have conveyed a different meaning than your words.

3. You may have negated your message by sugar-coating it on the front or by letting the other off the hook, saying afterwards that it is not all that important.

4. You may have ended up in an argument by not actively listening after your message.

5. You may have run into one of those rare individuals who is oblivious to his or her effect on others.

Defensive Responses to the Confrontation

1. Refuses to discuss it.

2. Only hears what he or she wants to hear.

3. Lets the confronter know that he or she isn't perfect either.

4. Tries to get the confronter to change his or her mind.

5. Merely rejects the confrontation.

6. Tries to get others on his or her side.

7. Immediately agrees with the confronter in an effort to get them off their back.

When Others Confront You, Respond Creatively to That Confrontation:

1. Understand the confronter.
2. Clarify the confrontation. Be sure you are clear about what they are trying to say.
3. Explore the confrontation. Ask questions and see if there is something else.
4. Take on manageable portions of the problem.
5. Commit yourself to take action.
6. Pray a lot.

45

A Matrix for Understanding Conflict

Effective confrontation is telling another person the effect that his or her behavior has on you.

The goal of confrontation is to get your own needs met without the other person becoming and remaining defensive.

☐ Intrapersonal Conflict
☐ Interpersonal Conflict
☐ Small Group Conflict
☐ Large Group Conflict
☐ Inter-group Conflict

☐ Space
☐ Schedules
☐ Methods
☐ Procedures
☐ Personal Preference
☐ Traditions
☐ Customs
☐ Values
☐ Beliefs
☐ Other_____

Power

Who is more powerful?

Acts of aggression / Withholding benefits / Neither is sure how far the other party will take the attack or withdrawal

Rights

Who is right and by what standard?

Agreed-upon rules / Contracts / Minutes / Precedent / Equality / Seniority

Reconcile Interests

What needs / values / concerns / fears / desires?

1. For every interest there usually exist several possible positions that could satisfy it.
2. Behind opposed positions lie many more compatible interests than conflicting ones.

No great advance has ever been made in science, politics, or religion, without conflict.
Conflict can be an opportunity for growth or the tool for destruction of relationships.

We do well to remind ourselves that anxiety signifies a conflict, and so long as conflict is going on, a constructive solution is possible.

Intrapersonal

This area involves conflicts and personal problems that individuals have within their own lives. Examples of this would include low self-image, shyness, pride, lack of patience, quick temper, depression, and anxiety.

Interpersonal

This area involves conflicts between two people. It could be between husband and wife, employer and employee, parent and child, relative and relative, friend and friend, or stranger and stranger.

Small Group

This area involves small groups of people who are at variance with each other. It could include interoffice departments, church groups, community groups, and competitors in business and educational institutions.

Large Group

This area involves conflict with larger collections of people, such as the Republicans versus the Democrats, federal employees versus private business, and/or labor unions. It could include states' rights versus federal laws.

Inter-group

This area involves conflict on a grand scale. This could include one country against another country. It could be a group of countries against another group of countries. *As conflict escalates from Intrapersonal to Intergroup, it could manifest itself as war.*

Space

This refers to an infringement of territorial space. It could include invasion of physical space, an invasion of responsibilities, or an invasion of area of supervision.

Schedules

This refers to a conflict of individual schedules and deadlines between two people or between groups of people.

Methods

This refers to how individual people approach the tasks before them. Not everyone works at the same pace or has the same ideas how a task should be accomplished.

Procedures

This refers to a set of established forms or methods for conducting business. There is often disagreement as to these steps and the course of action to be taken.

Personal Preference

This refers to your own personal taste, style, or opinion as to how a task should be done and the time it takes. It often comes down to simply not wanting to follow what is suggested.

Traditions

This refers to a body of unwritten precepts that have been

time-honored within the group or organization. Violating these traditions threatens the group.

Customs

This refers to a long-established practice or duty carried out by individuals within a group. This habitual practice often has the force of law or censure.

Values

This refers to strongly held ideals, principles, and standards that are highly prized by the individual of the group. People are willing to go to war over the things they value.

Beliefs

This refers to strongly held convictions by the individual or the group. Belief takes traditions, customs, and values to the final step. The individual or the group is willing to die for what they believe. *As conflict escalates from Space to Beliefs, it could manifest itself in a fight to the death.*

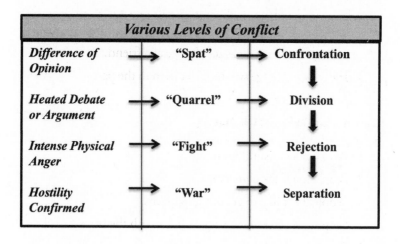

46

Dealing with Change

- People are looking for a leader, and change begins with the leader.
- Change is the price we pay for growth.
- All change does not represent progress, but if we do not change there will be no progress.

Three Attitudes Toward Change

1. The future will not be like the past.
2. The future will not be like what you expect. Change is coming so fast that few changes will turn out the way we project. We must embrace change as a friend.
3. The rate of change will be faster than in the past.

Reasons People Resist Change

1. People may misunderstand.
2. People may lack ownership.
3. People don't like to get out of patterns.
4. People may feel that change is not worth the price.
5. People may feel threatened with loss of something that is valuable to them...security, money, or control.
6. People may be satisfied with the old ways.

7. People may have a negative attitude toward change in general. Too much work.

8. There is a lack of respect for the leader.

9. People like tradition: We've never done it that way before.

10. People are afraid of the unknown.

Formula for Change

1. *The Change Agent*

   a. Is this idea mine or God's?

   b. Am I willing to pay the price this change will require?

   c. Whom will I lose? With every change you will lose someone.

   d. How long will it take?

   e. Will I be around after the change is made?

2. *The Main Person*—the individual responsible for the change

   a. Give them the vision.

   b. Give them the ownership.

   c. Give them the support.

   d. Give them time—help them to move forward together.

3. *Decision Makers*—people of influence

   a. When you've got it going for you, bring them together.

   b. When you've got it going against you, deal with them separately. Don't let them get together to kill change.

4. *The People Affected by Change*

   a. Ask for input.

   b. Appeal to their interests.

   c. Allow them concession for their needs whenever possible.

5. *The People*—resistance is always greatest when change comes as a surprise.

Timing

1. The wrong decision at the wrong time is a disaster.
2. The wrong decision at the right time is a mistake.
3. The right decision at the wrong time is unacceptable.
4. The right decision at the right time leads to success.

47

Can-Do Attitudes

Can't Do	Can Do
We've never done it before.	We can be the first.
It's too complicated.	Let's look at it from a different angle.
We don't have the resources.	Necessity is the Mother of Invention.
It will never work.	We'll give it a try.
There's not enough time.	We'll reevaluate some priorities.
We already tried it.	We learned from the experience.
There's no way it'll work.	We can make it work.
It's a waste of time.	Think of the possibilities.
It's a waste of money.	The investment will be worth it.
We don't have the expertise.	Let's network with them who do.
We can't compete.	We'll get a jump on the competition.
Our vendors won't go for it.	Let's show them the opportunities.
It's good enough.	There is always room for improvement.
We don't have enough money.	Maybe there's something we can cut.
We're understaffed.	We're a lean, mean machine.
We don't have enough room.	Temporary space may be an option.
It will never fly.	We'll never know until we try.
We don't have the equipment.	Maybe we can sub it out.
It's not going to be any better.	We'll try it one more time.
It can't be done.	It'll be a challenge.
No one communicates.	Let's open the channels.
I don't have any idea.	I will come up with alternatives.
Let somebody else deal with it.	I'm ready to learn something new.
We're always changing direction.	We're in touch with our customers.

The change is too radical.	Let's take a chance.
It takes too long for approval.	We'll walk it through the system.
Our customers won't buy it.	We'll do better at educating them.
It doesn't fit us.	We should look at it.
It's contrary to policy.	Anything is possible.
It's not my job.	I'll be glad to take the responsibility.
I Can't	I Can

48

Organizational Culture

- What are the unspoken rules in the culture regarding honesty and empathy?

- How are these rules learned, communicated, and changed?

- When are these behaviors considered appropriate or inappropriate?

- Which behaviors are rewarded? Which are punished?

- What topics can and cannot be discussed?

- When is it considered inappropriate to be honest or empathetic?

- What do people do when there are problems or conflicts?

- Which problems or conflicts are swept under the rug?

- How do people finally end up resolving their conflicts?

- How are intense emotions expressed and responded to?

- How do people respond to difficulties, glitches, and failures?

- What messages do leaders communicate through their behaviors?

- What do people believe about their power to change behaviors?

- How is the social climate generally viewed: happy, okay, or unhappy?

49

Pride and Humility

Proud, Unbroken People	Humble, Broken People
Focus on the failure of others	Overwhelmed with sense of their own spiritual need
Self-righteous; have a critical, fault-finding spirit; look at own life & fault through a telescope but others with a microscope	Compassionate; forgiving; look for best in others
Look down on others	Esteem all others better than self
Independent self-sufficient spirit	Dependent spirit; recognizes need for others
Maintain control; must be *my* way	Surrender control
Have to prove that they are right	Willing to yield the right to be right
Claim rights	Yield rights
Demanding spirit	Giving spirit
Self-protective of time, rights	Self-denying reputation
Desire to be served	Motivated to serve others
Desire to be a success	Desire to be faithful to make others a success
Desire for self-advancement	Desire to promote others
Driven to be recognized and appreciated	Sense of unworthiness; thrilled to be used at all; eager for others to get credit
Wounded when others are pro-moted, yet they are overlooked	Rejoice when others are lifted up
"The ministry is privileged to have me!"	"I don't deserve to serve in this ministry."

Think of what they can do for God	Know that they have nothing to offer God
Feel confident in how much they know	Humbled by how much they have to learn
Self-conscious	Not concerned with self at all
Keep people at arm's length	Risk getting close to others; willing to take risks in loving intimately
Quick to blame others	Accept personal responsibility—can see where they were wrong
Very concerned with who is right	Very concerned with what is right
Looks down on those who aren't as "spiritual" or "committed" as they are	Realizes that only God knows a person's true motives
Seeks to win arguments	Seeks peace and to win people

Humility isn't denying your strengths;
it's being honest about your weaknesses.

~ RICK WARREN

When you've done something wrong admit it, and be sorry.
No one in history has ever choked to death
from swallowing his pride.
Sometimes you have to shut up,
swallow your pride, and accept that you're wrong.
It's not giving up; it's growing up.

ANONYMOUS

50

A Broken Leader

- Am I willing to let go of my dreams and ambitions if such is God's will?

- Am I defensive when accused, criticized, or misunderstood?

- Am I coveting what others have, instead of waiting for heaven's rewards?

- Am I forgiving when offended, with or without apology?

- Am I complaining or arguing because of rights I've not yet surrendered?

- Am I thinking first of others out of love?

- Am I proud, appearing as though I am always right or know all the answers?

- Am I practicing the spiritual disciplines (prayer, fasting, solitude, simplicity, reading the Word of God, fellowshipping with other believers, and sharing the faith)?

- Am I silent regarding self-promotion, letting God handle my public relations?

- Am I daily saying, "God, whatever it takes, I'm willing to submit to Your leadership"?

- Am I expressing joy in the difficulties that serve to refine me?

- Am I taking risks out of obedience to Christ instead of giving in to fear, pride, anger, or denial?

  And He said to all, If any person wills to come after Me, let him deny himself [disown himself, forget, lose sight of himself and his own interests, refuse and give up himself] and take up his cross daily and follow Me [cleave steadfastly to Me, conform wholly to My example in living and, if need be, in dying also] (Luke 9:23 AMPC).

51

Accentuating the Positive

Negative	They talk too much.
Positive	They are friendly and put everyone at ease.
Negative	They argue so much.
Positive	They have strong convictions.
Negative	They think they know it all.
Positive	They are quite intelligent.
Negative	They are conceited.
Positive	They have confidence in themselves.
Negative	They are too easygoing.
Positive	They have a calming effect on everyone.
Negative	They are stingy.
Positive	They are trying to save money for our future.
Negative	They spend too much money.
Positive	They are trying to improve our lifestyle.
Negative	They are too rigid.
Positive	They are very organized.
Negative	They can never sit still.
Positive	They have a lot of energy.
Negative	They are too emotional.
Positive	They are very sensitive.

Fix your thoughts on what is true and good and right. Think about things that are pure and lovely, and dwell on the fine, good things in others. Think about all you can praise God for and be glad about (Philippians 3:8 TLB).

52

God's Secret
for Attitude Change

Philippians 4:4-9 TLB

COMMAND Always be full of joy in the Lord; I say it again, rejoice!

COMMAND Let everyone see that you are unselfish and considerate in all you do.

MOTIVATION Remember that the Lord is coming soon.

COMMAND Don't worry about anything; instead, pray about everything; tell God your needs and don't forget to thank him for his answers.

A PROMISE If you do this you will experience God's peace,

A GUARANTEE which is far more wonderful than the human mind can understand. His peace will keep your thoughts and your hearts quiet and at rest as you trust in Christ Jesus.

CLOSING And now, dear brothers, as I close this letter,

THOUGHT let me say this one more thing:

COMMAND Fix your thoughts on what is true and good and right.

COMMAND Think about things that are pure and lovely, and dwell on the fine, good things in others.

COMMAND Think about all you can praise God for and be glad about.

COMMAND Keep putting into practice all you learned from me and saw me doing,

PROMISE and the God of peace will be with you.

> When a man is gloomy, everything seems to go wrong; when he is cheerful, everything seems right! (Proverbs 15:15 TLB).

53

Work as a Ministry

Warren and David Wiersbe in *Making Sense of the Ministry*

1. The foundation of ministry is CHARACTER.
2. The nature of ministry is SERVICE.
3. The motive of ministry is LOVE.
4. The measure of ministry is SACRIFICE.
5. The authority of ministry is SUBMISSION.
6. The purpose of ministry is to GLORIFY GOD.
7. The tools of ministry are the WORD OF GOD and PRAYER.
8. The privilege of the ministry is GROWTH.
9. The power of the ministry is the HOLY SPIRIT.
10. The model for ministry is JESUS CHRIST.

54

Job or Ministry?

- If you are doing your work because no one else will, it is a JOB. If you are doing your work because you want to serve the Lord, it is a MINISTRY.

- If you are doing your work just well enough to get by, it is a JOB. If you are doing your work to the best of your ability, it is a MINISTRY.

- If you quit because someone criticizes you, it is a JOB. If you continue serving amidst stress, it is a MINISTRY.

- If you will do your work only as long as it doesn't interfere with your activities, it is a JOB. If you are committed to staying with it even when it means letting go of other things, it is a MINISTRY.

- If you quit because no one ever praises you or thanks you, it is a JOB. If you stay with it even though no one notices your effort, it is a MINISTRY.

- If you do your work because someone else said it needs to be done, it is a JOB. If you do your work because you think it needs to be done, it is a MINISTRY.

- If you find it hard to get excited about your work, it is a JOB. It is almost impossible not to get excited about a MINISTRY.

- Most businesses are filled with people doing a JOB. Serving others should be filled with people who are involved in a MINISTRY.

- If your concern is success and acknowledgement, it is a JOB. If your concern is faithfulness and serving, it is a MINISTRY.

- People might say, "Good job," when you do your JOB. The Lord will say, "Well done, you good and faithful servant," when you complete your MINISTRY.

- A JOB is your choice. A MINISTRY is something Christ wants you to do.

- In a JOB you give something to get something. In a MINISTRY you return something that has already been given to you.

- A JOB depends on your abilities. A MINISTRY depends on your availability to God.

- A JOB done well brings you praise. A MINISTRY done well brings honor and glory to CHRIST.

If God would grant us the vision,
the word "sacrifice" would disappear from our lips and thoughts.
We would hate things that now seem dear to us,
our lives would be suddenly too short.
We would despise time robbing distractions,
and charge the enemy with all our energy in the name of Christ.

~ NATE SAINT

55

Godly Leadership

OUT—To Be Done Away With	IN—To Be Put Into Practice
Gossip	Truthfulness
Bitterness	Forgiveness
Sowing Discord	Loyalty
Guarding Territory	Keeping Unity
Talking Behind Back	Support of Each Other
Pettiness	Grace
Legalism	Grace
Jealousy	Trust
Animosity	Love
Lone Rangers	Team Players
Laziness	High Energy
Content	Students
Complacent	Stretching
Status Quo	Change
Stagnant	Growth
Closed	Open
Departmental Focus	Big Picture
Small Thinking	Large Thinking
Conflict	Cooperation
Immaturity	Growing Up
Whining	Endurance
Negative Attitude	Positive Attitude
Prideful	Humility
Power Grabbing	Servant's Heart
Ungodliness	Godliness

56

Eight Signs You're Called to Be a Christian Leader

—George Barna, used by permission

1. ***Sensing the call.*** If you truly have been called, you will have a sense of divine selection for the task. You will have an inner conviction that, as amazing as it may seem, God wants you to lead people for Him and to Him.

2. ***Undeniable inclination.*** True leaders are naturally inclined to lead. Sometimes they assume a position of leadership reluctantly, as in the case of Timothy or Nehemiah. A person may either be drawn into leadership or have a natural enthusiasm and enjoyment for leadership. Ultimately, though, the urge or felt need to serve as a leader is undeniable.

3. ***Mind of a leader.*** A leader thinks differently from others. Leaders, being people of vision, are focused on the future. They think about the long-term implication of today's opportunities and choices. They are mindful of the big picture, not satisfied with focusing only on the microlevel events of the day.

4. ***Discernible influence.*** A true leader is one whose life bears the fruit of effective leadership. If you have been called by God, He will manifest that call by giving you tangible evidence of a special gift to lead. The accumulation of evidence that you have the ability to change the way individuals or groups think, speak, and live is one of God's

means of convicting you of the call and encouraging you to persist despite hardships.

5. *The company of leaders.* People are most comfortable around others who are like themselves. I have found that most leaders like to hang out with other leaders. They speak the same language. They resonate with the same issues and struggles. Being in the presence of other leaders defines the comfort zone of one called to lead.

6. *External encouragement.* One way of knowing if you are called to be a leader of God's people is whether you receive affirmation from other people. Such affirmation is most noteworthy when it comes from other true leaders. Leaders know their own kind; they know what it takes and what it looks like. If they sense the call in you, listen to their words.

7. *Internal strength.* Surprisingly few people have the internal strength to stand up for what is right. We call this courage. God's leaders are always people of great courage. If you are comfortable taking reasonable risks, traversing uncharted territory, and do not flinch at the prospect of taking the heat for the decisions you have made, you may well have the inner stuff God provides to those who are called to lead His people.

8. *Loving it.* Leading people is rarely a joyride. God's leaders—yes, even those called by Him—endure incredible amounts of heartache, controversy and animosity. If you have received that warm, tingling feeling of victory, a sense that all the hardships were worth the outcome, you know what a called leader experiences in the trenches of the spiritual battle.

57

How the Lord Leads

—A.W. Tozer, used by permission of the
Christian and Missionary Alliance

One of the problems most frequently encountered by serious-minded Christians is how to discover the will of God in a given situation.

This is not a small matter. To countless thousands of Christians it is vitally important. Their peace of heart depends upon knowing that God is guiding them and their failure to be sure that He is destroys their inward tranquility and fills them with uncertainty and fear. They must get help if they are to regain their confidence. Here is a modest effort to provide some help.

First, it is essential that we be completely dedicated to God's high honor and surrendered to the Lordship of Jesus Christ. God will not lead us except for His own glory, and He cannot lead us if we resist His will. The shepherd cannot lead a stubborn sheep. The evil practice of using God must be abandoned. Instead of trying to employ God to achieve our ends we must submit ourselves joyously to God and let Him work through us to achieve His own ends.

Now, granted that we are wholly committed to God with every full intent to obey Him, we may expect actually to be led by Him. The Scriptures that teach this are so many that one scarcely knows where to begin quoting. It only remains for us to believe they mean what they say.

The many choices that we Christians must make from day to day involve only four kinds of things: Those concerning which God has said an emphatic *no*; those about which He has said an equally emphatic *yes*; those concerning which He wants to consult our own sanctified preferences, and those few and rare matters about which we cannot acquire enough information to permit us to make intelligent decisions and which for that reason require special guidance from the Lord to prevent us from making serious mistakes.

Regardless of what our "positive thinkers" have said, the Scriptures have much to say about things Christians are not to do. Every call to repentance is a call to negative as well as positive moral action. "Cease to do evil; learn to do well" is fair epitome of the moral teaching of the Bible.

Put this down as an unfailing rule: Never seek the leading of the Lord concerning an act that is forbidden in the Word of God. To do so is to convict ourselves of insincerity.

Again, prophet, psalmist, apostle, and our blessed Lord Himself join to point out the way of positive obedience. His yoke is easy, His burden is light, and He giveth more grace, so let this be the second rule: Never seek the leading of the Lord concerning an act that has been commanded in Scriptures.

Now, a happy truth too often overlooked in our anxious search for the will of God is that in the majority of decisions touching our earthly lives God expresses no choice but leaves everything to our own preference. Some Christians walk under a cloud of uncertainty, worrying about which profession they should enter, which car they should drive, which school they should attend, where they should live, and a dozen or score of other matters, when their Lord has set them free to follow their own personal bent, guided only by their love for Him and for their fellow men.

On the surface it appears more spiritual to seek God's leading than just to go ahead and do the obvious thing. But it is not. If God gave you a watch, would you honor Him more by asking Him for the time of day or by consulting the watch? If God gave a sailor a compass, would the sailor please God more by kneeling in a frenzy of prayer to persuade God to show him which way to go or by steering according to the compass?

God's will is that we be free to exercise our own intelligent choice. The shepherd will lead the sheep, but he does not wish to decide which tuft of grass the sheep shall nibble each moment. God is pleased when we are pleased. He wills that we be free as birds to soar and sing our Master's praise without anxiety. God's choice for us may not be one but any one of a score of possible choices. The man or woman who is wholly and joyously surrendered to Christ cannot make a wrong choice. Any choice will be the right one.

But what about those rare times when a great deal is at stake, we can discover no clear scriptural instruction and yet are forced to choose between two possible courses? In such a situation we have God's faithful promise to guide us aright. Here, for instance, are two passages from the Word of the Lord: "If any of you lack wisdom, let him ask of God, that giveth to all men liberally, and upbraideth not; and it shall be given him. But let him ask in faith nothing wavering" (James 1:5-6, KJV). "Thus saith the Lord, thy Redeemer, the Holy One of Israel; I am the Lord thy God which teacheth thee to profit, which leadeth thee by the way that thou shouldest go" (Isaiah 48:17, KJV).

Take your problem to the Lord. Remind Him of these promises. Then get up and do what looks best to you. Either choice will be right. God will not permit you to make a mistake.

About Author

Bob Phillips, PhD, is the cofounder of the Pointman Leadership Institute that has presented *Inspirational, Trustworthy Leadership & Anti-Corruption* seminars in over 70 countries worldwide. He is a licensed marriage and family counselor and is the former executive director for Hume Lake Christian Camps one of America's largest youth camping programs. He is also a *New York Times* bestselling author and has written over 130 books on various topics. Among the titles are: The Babylon Rising Series, *How to Deal with Annoying People, Overcoming Anxiety and Depression, Great Thoughts and Funny Sayings, Overcoming Conflict, Heavenly Humor, Optimal Health and Wellness,* and *Headache Relief at Your Fingertips.* His most recent book is *Winning the Cancer Battle.*

Overcoming Conflict

Conflict is an unavoidable part of life, but you can control how you respond to it. You can let difficult situations fuel your anger and stir your desire to retaliate—or you can choose to grow in empathy, honesty, and acceptance. It's up to you.

Overcoming Conflict will give you the confidence you need to solve arguments, settle disputes, and restore harmony. You'll learn...

- ten common myths about conflict
- how to properly discuss differences and issues
- the importance of observing body language
- what to do when someone confronts you
- the power and meaning of forgiveness

By applying the principles in this book, you will develop new patterns of behavior that will significantly improve your personal and professional relationships and give you greater peace of mind when conflicts arise.

How to Deal with Annoying People

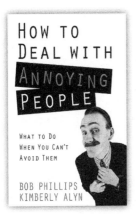

Everyone knows the world is filled with annoying people. Family counselor Bob Phillips and inspirational speaker Kimberly Alyn offer help to those needing to improve their personal and professional relationships. They are two friends who have devoted many years to speaking, teaching, and consulting on this important topic.

Churches, individuals, couples, employees, and managers will benefit from this look at personality styles and close—sometimes conflicted—interaction. Readers will discover why they are annoyed by others, why others are annoyed by them, and what they can do to create wholesome relationships. They'll learn to employ biblical principles along with a fun and simple process of identifying social cues. The result will be an immediate improvement in relating to the significant people in their lives.

Overcoming Anxiety and Depression

Anxiety and depression are the two most common emotions that plague people, causing emotional distress and feelings of inferiority, loneliness, and despair. Help is available for these people in pain—help from God, from His Word, and from the experience of gifted men and women who seek to lead people to wholeness.

Readers will readily identify with licensed family counselor Bob Phillips as he provides descriptions of the potentially debilitating effects of these difficult emotions. He reveals the root causes of anxiety and depression, which are fear and anger, and he helps readers acknowledge and deal with these driving forces in an effective, godly way. He includes a gentle and helpful presentation of spiritual issues and the gospel that will benefit believers and nonbelievers alike.

This hands-on, user-friendly approach is written with the lay person in mind and includes plenty of practical and effective self-help exercises that readers can use to find freedom. Christian counselors will recognize that Bob's system is built on a solid foundation of scriptural principles and up-to-date technical research on mental health.

To learn more about Harvest House books and
to read sample chapters, visit our website:

www.harvesthousepublishers.com

HARVEST HOUSE PUBLISHERS
EUGENE, OREGON